AF406111

THE PROBLEM WITH GROWING UP

CONFRONTING IMPOSTER SYNDROME

Also by Roddy Carter

BodyWHealth: Journey to Abundance

Sunset Lessons: Reflections on Light and Love from the Darkest of Places

Fireside Wisdom: Conversations to Inspire Personal Mastery

The Problem With Anger: And How to Solve It

Becoming Unstoppable: Your Neurocentric Coaching Guide to Achieving Unstoppable Success

The Serpent Within: Navigating Fear to Restore Inner Harmony

Little Book Series
Unstoppable Starts Here: A Short Guide to Mastering Your Brain and Unlocking Your Life
Greatness Awakened: A Short Guide to Mastering Your Complex Brain and Unlocking Your Best SELF

Unstoppable You Online Courses
Unstoppable You
Unstoppable You Business
Unleash Unstoppable
Unleash Success

Visit www.roddycarter.com for the full collection of Roddy's writing,
including new and forthcoming titles.

THE PROBLEM WITH GROWING UP

CONFRONTING IMPOSTER SYNDROME

by Roddy Carter, MD

Illustrated by Hannah Mae Silcock

Aquila Life Science Press
La Jolla, California

FIRST AQUILA LIFE SCIENCE PRESS EDITION, APRIL 2026
Published by Aquila Life Science, LLC, La Jolla, CA

THE PROBLEM WITH GROWING UP.

ISBN: 979-8-9990257-2-2

Printed in the United States of America

For every fractured being

who feels less than they are

and strives relentlessly to become whole.

ACKNOWLEDGEMENTS

To all who read these pages:

I have had the privilege of living and working with extraordinary people—brilliant minds, deep hearts—who have built magnificent lives on top of quiet self-doubt. Those who feel the most fragmented often also discover the most profound wholeness inside them. If you've ever felt small, unseen, or secretly less than, please know this: I see your greatness. It is my life's work and deepest joy to help you rediscover it. This book is for you.

To Sarah Dawson:

Your fierce loyalty to truth in language remains one of the great gifts of my professional life. With unmatched sensitivity and precision, you continue to help me refine every word until it becomes a clear vessel for meaning. You are so much more than an exceptional editor—you are a trusted guardian of voice and vision. Thank you for walking this road with me, again.

To Hannah Mae Silcock:

Once more, your artistry has revealed the emotional undercurrents of this work with tender grace and power. Your illustrations expand the story, lending rich form and color to the architecture of transformation. You have exquisitely captured what lies between the words, and I'm forever grateful.

PREFACE

I've been called confident, even fearless. For most of my adult life, I've held positions of responsibility and authority: leading teams, shaping strategy, and inspiring growth and achievement in others.

From the outside, it always looked like I had it all together, maybe even like I had arrived.

But I remember a moment, high on the ladder of my business career, when a colleague attacked me with words that I'll never forget: "You don't fill your shoes."

They hit like a lightning bolt, partly because they were intended to hurt but mainly because they touched something already alive inside me—a whisper of doubt that had been growing for years.

I smiled on the outside. But inside, I shrank.

The comment pierced the image I had curated of myself. And in its wake, I began to ask deeper questions: "Who am I, really? Why do I feel this way, when everything on paper suggests otherwise? And what if I'm not alone in this?"

As it turns out, I wasn't alone.

In the years that followed, I worked with hundreds—eventually thousands—of high-functioning, accomplished leaders: people who were admired, successful, even beloved...and yet quietly felt like they didn't measure up.

They wore masks. They felt fragmented. And, just like me, they carried the silent ache of being *less than*.

This book is for them. And it's for you.

The Problem With Growing Up is a guide to the imposter story that lives in us all. It draws from neuroscience, my own experience, and those I've walked alongside. It explores how our brains build identity, how we protect ourselves from pain, and how—paradoxically—our greatest strengths become our greatest stumbling blocks.

In this book, you will learn that imposter syndrome is not weakness or psychological frailty; it's biology, a universal phenomenon rooted in our natural design.

More than anything, this book is a path to wholeness.

If you have ever doubted that you are enough, questioned your belonging, or felt like you were living behind a performance, please hear this: You are not broken. You are not alone. And there is a way forward.

This is not a self-help book. It's a mirror, a map, and a quiet companion on your journey back to your SELF.

Welcome to *The Problem With Growing Up*.

Let's walk forward together.

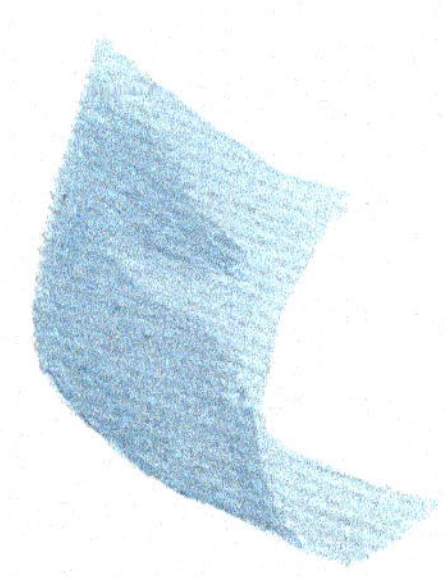

THE STORY OF GROWING UP

Daniel slid into the back seat of the Uber and let the door click shut behind him. The tinted windows held back the city's chaos, but not the thoughts racing in his mind.

He stared out as the white dome of the Capitol faded into the distance.

The hearing had gone well, by every measure.

He had held the attention of some of the sharpest minds in the world. His testimony on artificial intelligence had landed exactly as he'd hoped. Everyone else had focused on the risks of the technology itself, but Daniel had shifted the spotlight:

"The danger isn't the AI; it's the humans who will use it. This will be the greatest invention in history...but only if we remain the masters of our own minds."

It had stopped the room. A few skeptical looks, then slow nods. One senator had leaned forward, eyes narrowed. "So you're saying we don't need better computers. We need better people?"

Daniel had smiled, just enough. "Exactly. Prepare them. Empower them. That's how we make this work."

The car turned toward his hotel, headlights tracing the glass of the National Gallery. He let himself feel proud for a moment.

But then, as always, the voice crept in.

"You don't belong in that room. They were just being polite. Sooner or later, they'll see through you."

Daniel clenched his jaw, shut his eyes, and dismissed the unwelcome intruder. He had work to do.

Back in his hotel, he loosened his tie and dropped onto the edge of the bed. The room hummed with quiet luxury.

He pulled his laptop toward him and opened it. There was a new email near the top of his inbox.

    Invitation: The Stratos Inner Circle

His pulse skipped as he clicked.

The message was concise.

    You've been selected to join the Stratos Inner Circle, a carefully curated fellowship of global visionaries shaping the world.

His pulse beat faster. He'd heard of this organization. Only seven members, new each year, all under age 40. And each one a well-known name. Architects of industries. Changemakers.

He stared at the screen for a long moment. That same whisper stirred again: *"What if they made a mistake, inviting you?"*

He shook his head. There was no space for doubt. Not tonight.

He clicked Accept.

And with that single click, Daniel crossed an invisible threshold—into the orbit of seven remarkable strangers and into an experience that would quietly alter the course of his life.

The Stratos Inner Circle

This is not a place to prove yourself. You've already done that.

This is a place to rise—above the noise, beyond the now—to explore the Worldmaker within you.

This is a curated global fellowship for leaders under 40, visionaries who have already reshaped their industries, cultures, and communities.

Stratos is not about outward accomplishment. It's about what follows.

Confront the deeper questions that emerge when excellence is no longer the goal, but the given.

Over the course of a year, the Circle gathers in iconic global locations at the intersection of history and horizon. From mountaintops to moorlands, each immersive retreat is designed to dismantle, awaken, and transcend.

This is not just a fellowship. This is a threshold.

THE STRATOS

INNER CIRCLE

INTRODUCING THIS YEAR'S MEMBERS

DANIEL HAYES

Silicon Valley, California, USA (Born in Monterey, California, USA)
Global Advisor on AI, Ethics, & Systems Design

A tech prodigy who sold two startups before age 30, Daniel now advises world leaders on the future of technology and humanity. An internationally respected thought leader in artificial intelligence, ethics, and global governance, he is admired for his intellect, clarity, and calm authority. He is known as both a systems architect and a moral compass for a rapidly changing world.

New York City, New York, USA (Born in Recife, Brazil)
Director of Global Child Protection Initiatives, UNICEF USA

A globally recognized advocate for youth justice and child protection, Rafael leads bold initiatives at the intersection of policy, storytelling, and grassroots activism. He is known for his passionate voice, magnetic presence, and ability to bridge worlds—from UN chambers to the communities he serves. He is a force for dignity, equity, and lasting change.

RAFAEL MOREIRA

LIAM MURPHY

Cork, Ireland (Born in Cork, Ireland)
International Lawyer & Conflict Resolution Expert

A trusted figure in global diplomacy, Liam mediates complex negotiations across political, corporate, and humanitarian sectors. Revered for his intellect and warmth, he brings sharp strategy and deep empathy to every table. Known as the calm in the storm, he carries both legacy and leadership with disarming grace.

Kyoto, Japan (Born in Kyoto, Japan)
Cultural Philosopher & Curator of Intangible Heritage

Renowned for her luminous essays and quiet authority, Sora advises global institutions on cultural meaning, memory, and ethical aesthetics. A still presence in volatile spaces, she is respected as a guardian of wisdom, beauty, and ancestral continuity.

SORA TAKAHASHI

Leipzig, Germany (Born in Ratzeburg, Germany)
Founder, Second Wind Initiative | Olympic Gold Medalist & Environmental Strategist

A three-time Olympic champion and environmental innovator, Olga leads a global youth movement uniting sport and climate justice. Renowned for her composure, stamina, and moral clarity, she is both respected and quietly formidable. She is a reformer who brings athletic precision to the world's most urgent environmental challenges.

OLGA SCHÄFER

AWA VALANTIN

Geneva, Switzerland (Born in Saint-Louis, Senegal)
Biomedical Engineer & Global Advisor on Neurotechnology and Equity

Globally recognized for her groundbreaking work in neuro-integrative prosthetics, Awa is the youngest female recipient of the Lasker Award. Advising on the intersection of neuroscience, technology, and medical justice, she is admired for her precision, composure, and quiet power. She brings brilliance and deep moral clarity to the future of human advancement.

ALEXEI VOLKOV

St. Petersburg, Russia (Born in St. Petersburg, Russia)
Founder & CEO, QuantumEdge Research Institute

A pioneer in algorithmic finance, Alexei leads one of the world's most sophisticated digital investment platforms. Renowned for his logic, restraint, and predictive brilliance, he is both admired and enigmatic. He is a strategist who sees logical systems where others see chaos.

Cape Town,
South Africa

Edinburgh,
Scotland

Sedona,
United States

Athens,
Greece

Rio de Janeiro,
Brazil

Mount Fuji,
Japan

MEETING LOCATIONS

Six months later, his plane touched down in Paris. The famous city glowed, its elegance whispering what no voice needed to say.

A few hours later, he stood in the backstage shadows, looking up at the bright lights that glared down at him through the deep red of the stage curtain. This was the biggest night of his life: an international ceremony, his name etched among the honored few joining the Circle.

Beyond the curtain, the room shimmered with brilliance as intellectual icons and influencers from every corner of the globe gathered in quiet recognition. The master of ceremonies read through Daniel's credentials and invited him to step forward.

He trembled. A mixture of excitement and fear pulsed through his veins as deafening applause erupted.

He straightened his shoulders to step forward and heard something inside him whisper, *"They're all someone, each a legend in their own worlds, and I'm just a boy in borrowed clothes."*

Daniel hardly slept on the overnight flight to Cape Town, at the southern tip of Africa.

Upon arrival, their morning began before sunrise. At the foot of Table Mountain, Daniel joined his peers—strangers in name, though not in spirit.

They climbed in quiet rhythm, the world still sleeping below.

At the summit, words gave way to wonder. Laughter warmed the air. Connections sparked.

On the descent, silence returned—this time sacred. The world stretched beneath them, bathed in light.

They had only just arrived, yet something ancient stirred between them. And in that quiet descent, a deeper knowing began to take root.

After breakfast, they gathered in a glass-walled room overlooking the sparkling ocean. Olga moved with silent precision, her stillness radiating power. Awa sat composed, her quiet authority wrapped in elegance and edge. Liam leaned back, sharp eyes softened by warmth and wit. Rafael couldn't sit still—his energy sparked like static. Sora poured tea without a sound, her presence as calm and exact as the motion itself. Alexei focused intently, solving unspoken problems.

Daniel smiled. Nodded. Matched their poise. But inside, he was still the boy who stood by the curtain.

The host entered with a warm smile. "Welcome to the Stratos Inner Circle Experience. This is not a place to prove yourself. You've already done that." She paused, letting the stillness deepen.

"This is a place to find yourself, to remember who you are beneath the trophies and titles."

She gestured to the center of the room, where there was a circle of chairs. "Your first invitation," she said, "is to tell your story. The real one. We want to know who you are."

A chill ran down Daniel's spine. He hadn't expected this. *What do I do now?* he wondered in slight panic. *They know the official version, and are impressed. If I tell them the whole truth, they'll change their minds.*

The room blurred. The voices faded. Daniel's mind drifted back to his childhood.

Six-year-old Daniel sat at the dining room table, his feet swinging clear of the floor. He clutched the piece of paper the school principal had presented him at the assembly—his first school award. The older children had clapped for the little boy who leaped forward to receive his recognition.

Looking up from his food, Daniel quietly explored his father's face with his eyes, searching for a sign of pride.

"Good work," his father said without looking up, nodding once before returning to his newspaper.

His mother smiled, but her attention was elsewhere.

A warmth flickered inside him—brief, barely perceptible, then gone.

He had grown to understand: Love and attention had to be earned.

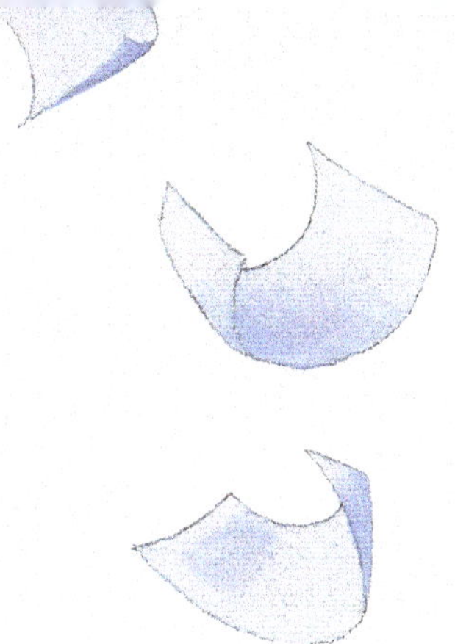

That night, he placed his certificate under the lamp on the table next to his bed. He would collect them, he decided. Proof that he was enough. He would soon have so many that his father would *have* to be proud of him.

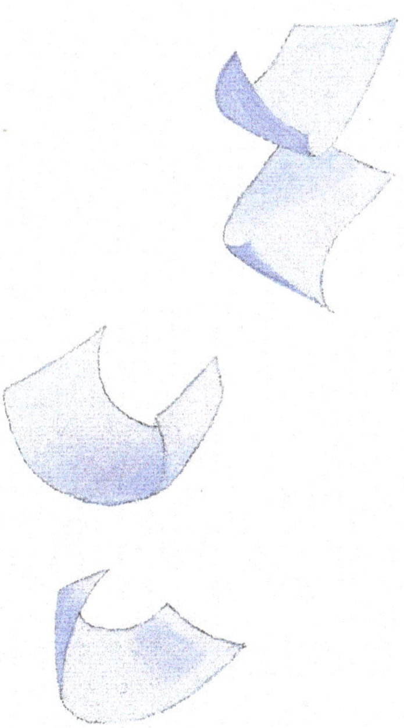

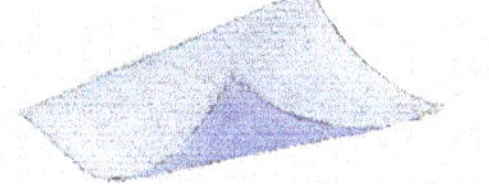

Two years later, he sat in a big hall, a finalist in the county spelling bee.

He faced the audience as the pronouncer asked him to spell one more tricky word. It was the single-elimination phase, and only one other finalist remained.

A pained sigh erupted from the adults in the room. Daniel must have said something wrong. It turned out he had missed one letter, a silent K. He would finish in second place.

He felt his chest tighten as he walked to the back of the room and took a seat next to his best friend.

"Don't be a wimp," his friend prompted, digging his sharp elbow into Daniel's ribs.

Daniel laughed, fighting the sting in his eyes and forcing his face into a grin.

That night in bed, he whispered to himself, "Never let them see your pain."

Daniel was a smart, hardworking sixth-grader. Despite being younger than his peers, he achieved the top score in a very challenging science examination.

When he jumped into the car at the end of the school day and shared the news, his kind mother beamed. "What did you actually score, Daniel?"

"Ninety-eight percent," he responded, settling into the back seat.

"Where did you lose the two percent?" she asked. He looked out the window at the rain drops that had begun falling. *She wouldn't even understand if I told her*, he thought.

That night, as he lay in bed, he heard his parents speaking.

"He's smart," his father said. "But he needs to be sharper. He makes too many little mistakes."

Daniel turned on his lamp, picked up his pen, and began writing a list: *Ways to Be Better*.

By morning, his plan was set. No more mistakes. No more uncertainty. No more weakness.

Daniel's life started to change. He noticed that his body was shifting, beginning to take on the appearance of an older boy. He started to see the girls in his class differently.

In secret, he liked to dream and create art. He hid a treasured sketchbook filled with drawings in the bottom drawer of his desk. Late at night, while his parents stared at the TV in silence, he would bring out his colored pencils, sketching elegant webs of logic and light.

One day, he shared his drawings with a trusted teacher. "You have a powerful gift, Daniel," she declared.

He felt something light and warm in his chest, something that he hadn't ever experienced before.

That night, emboldened by his teacher's words, he brought the book to the dinner table.

His father glanced silently at the pages while he chewed. Daniel shifted anxiously in his chair, wishing he hadn't made this decision. Eventually, his father put down his knife and fork. "Nice enough, I suppose," he said, blandly. "But that won't get you anywhere."

Before going to bed, Daniel placed the sketchbook back in its hiding place, vowing to never open it again.

With his head on his pillow, he watched the shadows of the trees dancing on the walls and wished that one of them could forever hide his ridiculous dreamy creativity.

In his final year of high school, Daniel led his team to win a national debate competition.

When the winners were declared, the crowd erupted in wild applause. His teammates thronged him, and the audience stood, cheering loudly. They knew that it was he who had tipped the delicate balance in his team's favor.

Out of the corner of his eye, he saw his parents smiling broadly as the other parents congratulated them.

But deep inside, he felt nothing.

It felt like his smile had been stitched onto his face, but the thread didn't reach his heart.

He knew that he had done well, spoken powerfully, conveyed the closing arguments with passion and conviction. Or had he?

It had felt more like someone else. It felt like he wore a mask, and the mask had fused to his face. On the outside, he smiled and won debates. On the inside, he felt empty.

He had learned well. He had performed well—almost perfectly, in fact. He had hidden his weaknesses and focused everyone's attention on his strengths. They were happy. But still, he felt nothing.

And so, his life had gone from strength to strength. Each year he learned more, performed better, won more prizes. He graduated from college and was invited into a top doctoral program in computer science and business.

He didn't pursue his PhD, deciding instead to start his own company. At age 24, he sold it to a global powerhouse for many millions of dollars. He poured the proceeds into the next idea, building and selling a second company by the time he was 27.

He fell in love and got married. He and his wife had two beautiful children.

By every external marker, his life was perfect.

And one night, on his bed in a DC hotel room, he had opened the email inviting him to join this prestigious Circle. And that's how he got to stand there, looking out the window and wondering how he was going to share his truth with this extraordinary group.

Daniel blinked, pulled back into the present as it came to his turn to speak. He described how his parents had always encouraged him to excel and how he'd known the value of hard work at a young age. He shared the specifics of his career and knew he had performed well—he saw it in the others' eyes.

But beneath the polish, his mind was somewhere else entirely, lost in the question of how to show up as the real Daniel. Did he ever know who the "real Daniel" was anymore?

The rest of the day went by in a blur. As he left the hotel for the airport, he looked up into the blue skies. *How am I going to tell them who I really am?* he wondered. *Which story would I tell them, anyway? I've spent so long becoming what the world needs, I no longer actually know who I am.*

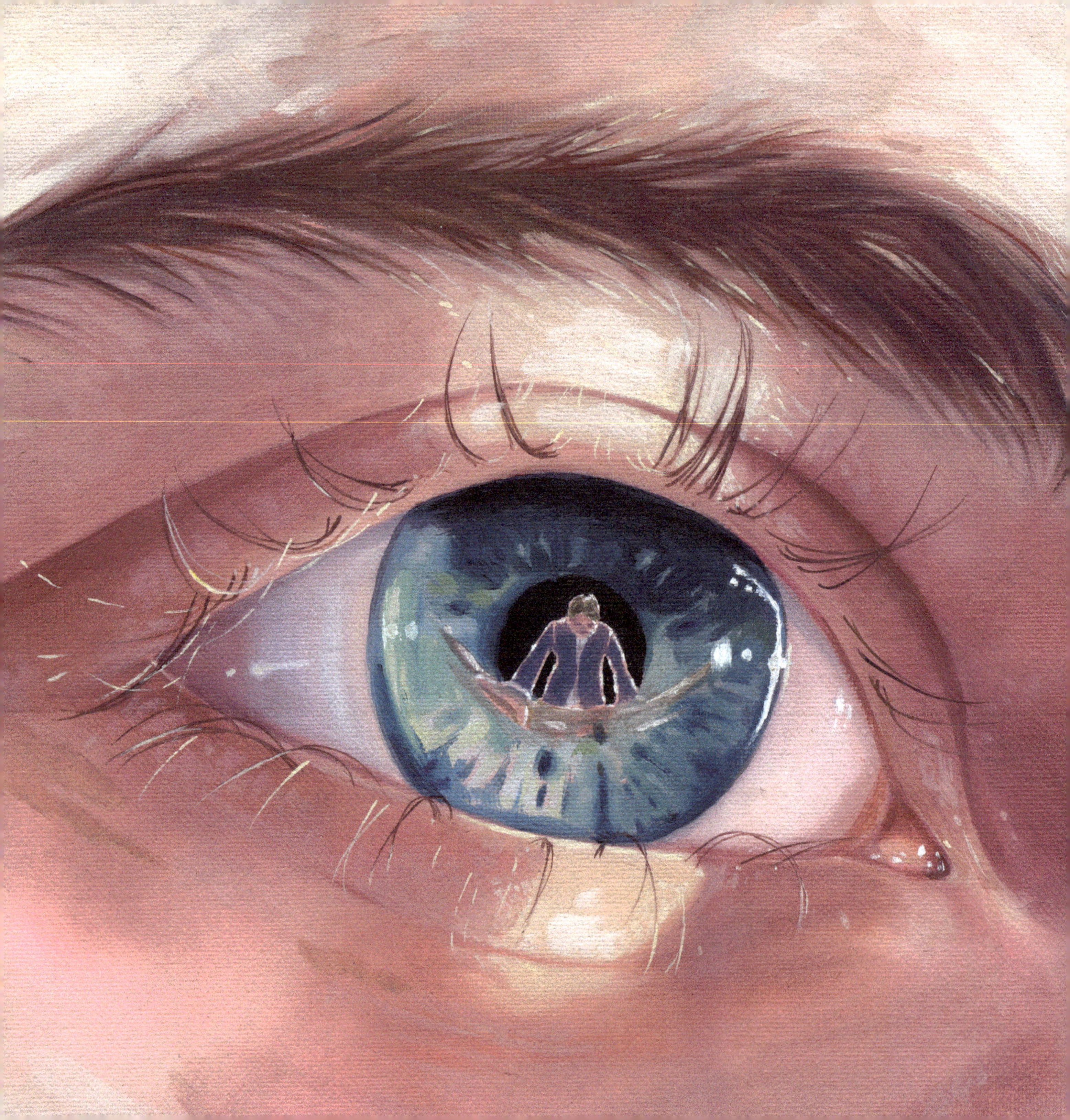

Daniel returned to his office in Silicon Valley. He was surprised to find that he struggled to concentrate on his work. He lay awake at night worrying about how he could hide his true story from his new friends.

As he'd stood on the stage in Paris, feeling like a little boy, his whole life had begun to crumble. How was he to sustain the façade of happiness and success?

At work, his team found him distracted and tense. They began to worry that something was going wrong in the business.

At home, his wife was concerned. He spent so many hours gazing into the distance, ignoring his children while they played in the next room. *Where has that beautiful man gone?* she wondered. *Where is the engaged and present husband and father?*

The night before he flew to Edinburgh for the next Inner Circle meeting, he finally confided in her. "I have been admitted to a special community of human beings. But I'm not sure I deserve to be there."

The fog didn't lift all day.

From the moment they arrived, Edinburgh wrapped them in gray silk. The city stood like a sentinel, ancient and solemn. Even the air felt older there, laced with memory and myth.

They gathered in a room in the old part of the city, the castle framed behind them like an impending question. Candles flickered beside quiet screens. Their breath was visible, with every word echoing just a little longer than expected.

They had grown familiar with each other now—names became voices, voices became glances, and glances became something harder to name. But unbeknownst to the others, each sat with a secret. No one had truly stepped into the inner circle.

Until Olga spoke.

"I've always known how to be strong," she said, her voice even. "How to row through pain. How to show up composed and powerful."

A few faces looked up in surprise. Olga never spoke first.

She continued, holding them in her piercing gaze. "But here...among you...I feel something I can't explain. At home, but...unprepared."

Her jaw twitched.

"I don't know how to *be* in a room like this. I've built a self the world applauds. But it's made of steel and silence."

She stopped. One hand clenched, then released.

"This is the strongest I've ever been. But I don't know how to be here."

The room felt suspended. In Daniel's mind, it was as if a great redwood had fallen—sudden, stunning. And yet, in the silence it left behind, something even larger had emerged.

Daniel stood slowly, then spoke—not to perform, not to prove, but to reveal.

"I've spent my whole life becoming who the world needed," he said. "Not a lie. Just...not the truth."

He took a deep breath.

"There's a table in my head where every decision is debated and dissected. The critic. The planner. The performer. The perfectionist.

"They helped me build an empire. But they don't help me find myself.

"I know how to win. I just don't know how to *be*.

"I am not broken. But I am lost. I need to find the real me."

The silence that followed wasn't empty; it was sacred. Around the circle, no one moved. No one breathed. It was as if they all recognized the moment: not a breakdown, but a breakthrough. A man not falling apart but finally seeing his true reflection in the mirror.

The air had changed, charged now with reverence. Something ancient had been named—something shared, though never spoken.

Awa was the first to respond. She sat still for a long moment, eyes downcast, hands folded. Then she leaned forward, fingers knotted. "Every time someone praises me," she whispered, "I flinch. Like they've mistaken me for someone else.

"I've spent my whole life perfecting everything: my work, my image, even my silence." Her voice was steady, but something inside her was trembling. "Usually, that impeccably polished complexion protects me. But in this circle it feels like glass: too thin to hide behind, too fragile to protect."

Liam gave a wry smile, then shook his head. "I'm usually the one making people laugh in rooms like this." He looked up, eyes tired but kind. "But here, that trick doesn't work. I'm not sure I'm needed. There's nothing to defuse. You're all so capable, even in your vulnerability."

He paused.

"I've built my whole identity on being the one who lightens the mood. But lately I wonder if that's just another way of disappearing. It used to give me purpose, but now it leaves me feeling peripheral—a little useful, but profoundly unseen."

Rafael leaned forward, elbows on his knees, fingers laced tight. "I'm usually the one who lights the match," he said. "The agitator. The change-maker. I walk into rooms ready to disrupt, to inspire. That's how I know I belong—when there's a battle to fight."

He exhaled. "But in here, no one needs rallying. There's nothing to fight against, no one to prove wrong. And without that edge"—his voice dropped—"I'm not sure I have any meaningful value.

"I've built my identity around motion, disruption, fire. Stillness feels like erasure. Without a cause to champion, I fear I'll disappear entirely."

Sora, barely audible, offered, "I am trained to hold space. To observe, dutifully. To listen deeply and let silence do the speaking.

"But lately, I wonder if I've mistaken silence for safety. If being unseen became my way of being accepted."

Alexei leaned back in his chair, arms crossed tightly, eyes narrowed in deep thoughtfulness. "When they took my father away, my mother cried. It scared me, so I left the room. I was seven."

He paused, eyes fixed on a distant point.

"Since then, I've led with intellect: analysis, strategy, precision, control. Flawless, unbreachable brilliance has been my armor. It's how I stay safe."

His voice lowered. "But in this room, that's not enough. There are no calculations to make, no agendas to predict. Without those weapons, I feel totally exposed." He glanced up briefly. "I feel like that terrified little boy who fled the room so many years ago."

Olga didn't speak again. She didn't need to. Her tears from earlier still shimmered in memory, louder than any words.

Her gaze met Daniel's. She nodded, a warrior acknowledging another soldier in the campaign for wholeness.

A stillness that felt like truth prevailed.

In the weeks that followed, something began to shift.

The façade had exploded. But instead of crumbling, each of them grew stronger. They had revealed the truth of their fragmented inner worlds, and in the same breath, each had glimpsed their true self. They moved forward together with new eyes.

No one rushed to fix anything. No one offered advice. They simply stayed present. And in that presence, healing began.

Between sessions, their lives resumed: boardrooms, courtrooms, lecture halls, and labs. But something was different. Beneath the performance, there was a quiet confidence, an observer awakened within. The voice asked them not *What should I do?* but *Who am I now, and what will I do?*

Back in the Circle, their work deepened. Feedback turned from polite to profound. No longer seeking to impress, they asked more probing questions—of themselves and of each other. *What am I hiding? What am I protecting? What would it mean to be truly seen?*

And the strangest thing happened.

The very strategies they had once used to survive—the perfectionism, the logic, the deflection, the relentless drive— were no longer enemies.They were recognized, with gratitude, as brilliant adaptations. Outdated, perhaps, but once life-saving.

The Taskmaster had once protected the vulnerable child. The Strategist had kept the peace in a hostile home. The Performer had earned the love that should have been unconditional. The Planner had ensured no vital detail was overlooked. The Perfectionist had built an exquisite façade to hide any weakness. The Critic had nitpicked so thoroughly that no outside criticism would ever hurt. The Fighter had chosen battles to ensure triumph. The Intellectual had analyzed and strategized, using calculation as armor.

Now these inner voices were thanked—and their persistent authority questioned.

And something more authentic emerged.

It didn't happen all at once. Some days were laced with fear; others were flighty and uplifting. Slowly, each member of the circle began to lead from a different place.

They had found, or were beginning to find, their true SELF: the steady, central core of their being that had been hidden behind the survival algorithms of their protective brains. They found the one who witnessed without panic. Who led without performing. Who connected fearlessly.

They were no longer just extraordinary achievers. They were integrating, becoming whole.

And together, they found something no accolade had ever given them: true self-worth.

They had entered the Circle as titans, architects of influence, paragons of purpose, each arriving with résumés gilded in brilliance, their reputations reverberating across industries, institutions, and nations.

But they would leave as something rarer: whole, reintegrated human beings.

They no longer needed to prove they belonged. They simply knew it.

Each of them had begun the journey as the best in the world at something. Now, they stepped forward with a new compass: full, authentic presence.

They would return to their spheres of influence—still powerful, still visionary—now leading from deep within. Not flawless, but free. Rooted. Real. Reclaimed.

They met one last time below the quiet slopes of Mount Fuji. There was no fanfare, just shared tea, wool scarves, and the hush of a mountain morning.

There was no concluding ceremony. Their graduation was not into a title or a role but into themselves, each now standing in their full power, with the quiet understanding that something irreversible had taken place.

They were **enough**.

And now, dear reader, it's just you and me.

We've journeyed alongside seven extraordinary individuals who lay down their brilliance long enough to find something even greater: themselves.

You've experienced their fears and their protective masks. Behind these, they discovered unimaginable treasures hidden within fractured inner worlds. They uncovered their truth.

And maybe—just maybe—you've felt something stir within you.

Before we get there, let me ask you:

If these paragons of success felt like imposters,
who among us is immune?

Not one of us escapes this phenomenon. Our brains, still running childhood code, *mistake survival for success*—keeping us safe but feeling small, long after we've outgrown the danger.

Now, if you're ready, I'm going to invite you to join the Circle in a journey of self-discovery. I'm going to show you the inherent biology of growing up and the path to freedom. I'm going to show you how to confront imposter syndrome, so that you too can find your true SELF and awaken to the life that's been gently waiting for you, rooted in peace, aligned with purpose, and alive with power.

AUTHOR'S NOTE

The journey to this book began not in a lab or a lecture hall but at the finish line of an Olympic race.

When I asked the elite athletes I was working with at the time what it felt like to win a gold medal, their answers stunned me. They spoke not of euphoria or chaos but of stillness, a kind of sacred silence. Amid the thunder of crowds and the roar of victory, they described a mind at rest—utterly focused, wholly present.

That silence haunted me. It was so different than the relentless chatter that filled my own mind.

Later, I faced a mid-career reckoning that forced me to confront that internal noise. I could no longer ignore the mental torment. I began to search for inner quiet. I wanted authority over my own mind. I wanted control, not through force but through understanding. I began a journey to end my inner suffering.

It wasn't until a few years later that, while working with my executive coaching clients, I began to notice something peculiar. In moments of emotional intensity, their tone, posture, and even facial expressions would shift. At times it felt as though I was speaking to a younger version of them: vulnerable, uncertain, and often overwhelmed.

Initially, I wondered if I was imagining it. But over time, the pattern became unmistakable. In those moments, it was as if a part of their earlier experience had stepped forward to speak. I began to engage with these parts, and the results were extraordinary. Clients would experience breakthroughs—not from analyzing their behavior but from speaking directly to the hidden selves driving it.

So began my deep dive into the phenomenon of sub-personalities, or "Parts." I found reflections of this truth everywhere: in the archetypes of Carl Jung,[1] in the voices of Gestalt therapy,[2] and in the trauma work of Bessel van der Kolk and his theory of arrested development.[3] I encountered it in Hal and Sidra Stone's Voice Dialogue[4] and Richard Schwartz's Internal Family Systems.[5,6] As I developed my own framework, I was gratified to see that we were converging on the same inner landscape, often using strikingly similar language. For a scientist, it was powerful validation. For an earnest seeker, it was nothing less than a homecoming.

Out of this journey emerged what I call the **Polymorphic Mind Model (PMM)**, a practical and compassionate way to understand the constellation of sub-personalities within us and to help each one find peace—not by silencing them but by allowing the true SELF to lead.

This book shares what I've learned through decades of clinical work, coaching practice, rigorous research, and my own personal journey. I do not offer it as dogma but as a humble invitation to inquiry. I am simply a pilgrim and pathfinder: honest, curious, and hungry for wholeness. I have used science as my scalpel and compassion as my compass.

And I have found something extraordinary: a quieter mind, a steadier joy, and a growing experience of inner peace.

This is not just the story of Olympic champions or high achievers. It is the story of all of us.

The following chapters will offer the science behind the story and the tools that have the power to transform your life.

Here is an overview of what's to come:

- Chapter 2: A brief overview of the overarching hypothesis that our brains fail to notice that we grow up

- Chapter 3: An explanation of the consequences of our brains running software from our childhood even as we continue into adulthood

- Chapter 4: An exploration of the path to reprogramming the brain

- Chapter 5: An outline of practical steps to reprogram the brain

- Chapter 6: An introduction to the various sub-personalities created in childhood

- Chapter 7: A call to personal transformation

Your true SELF is not lost. It is waiting.

Let's go find it.

THE PROBLEM WITH GROWING UP

As you'll discover throughout this book, the impact of our childhood on our adult experience is profound—biologically, emotionally, and behaviorally. But the problem with growing up is not just that childhood shapes us.

The real problem with growing up is actually quite simple: We're adults trying to thrive on toddler software. The brain fails to recalibrate after childhood, continuing to run neural algorithms designed to protect a powerless child—anachronistic codes that unconsciously reinforce the illusion that adults are still at risk, leaving capable humans feeling fragile and unworthy and sustaining maladaptive strategies ill suited for adult life.

Or, put more simply:

The brain code that once kept us safe now keeps us small.

Let me explain.

We are born physically helpless, biologically fragile, and entirely dependent on others for survival. In those early years, our brain's singular goal is to keep us alive. It achieves this by encoding powerful protective strategies: hypervigilance, people pleasing, suppression, overachievement, withdrawal, and more. These patterns are not random. They are intelligent adaptations designed to help us survive in a world we can't control.

And they work. When we're children, these protective algorithms succeed in keeping us safe, fed, and sometimes even loved.

But here's the catch: The brain doesn't automatically update when we grow up. Instead, those same survival codes continue to run silently in the background, guiding our choices, shaping our relationships, and, most importantly, defining how we see ourselves. And because they were created by a child—and *for* a child— they're no longer fit for our purposes.

We are now intelligent, competent adults, capable of influence, leadership, and love. But inside, we're still being guided by neural instructions that whisper, "Hey little boy, you're not safe." "Hey little girl, don't speak up." "Stay small." "Be perfect." "Don't make too much noise." "You don't deserve better."

The result? Even at the height of success, many of us feel inadequate, undeserving, or unseen. Despite evidence to the contrary, we still experience ourselves as fragile, trapped by internal rules that no longer apply to the world we live in.

And because these inner voices are shameful, we rarely speak of them. In fact, we keep them carefully hidden from others.

This is why so many high-functioning, high-achieving adults secretly suffer from imposter syndrome. It's not a failure of confidence; it's a consequence of normal neurobiology and a simple lack of neural recalibration.

So why *don't* we just recalibrate? For many reasons, ultimately. Most importantly, we're not taught about this. Not by anyone, ever! Also, by the time we reach adulthood, we're so identified with our protective algorithms that we cannot see them. We've probably even said ourselves, "That's just who I am."

Chronologically, we age. Biologically, we mature. Socially, we evolve.

But neurologically, emotionally, and psychologically? We often remain stuck, servant to our brain and its increasingly irrelevant advice.

Unless we wake up to the outdated scripts running our lives, we will keep mistaking survival for success and illusion for truth. We will keep asking our childhood brain to run our adult life.

But there is good news.

Because these patterns are learned, they can be unlearned. The brain can be reconditioned. These outdated strategies, once necessary, can be updated. And behind the protective Parts—the Critic, the Perfectionist, the Achiever—is something deeper, truer, and more whole.

That something is your Authentic SELF.

And in the pages ahead, I will help you meet and liberate your SELF.

CHAPTER 3

THE POLYMORPHIC MIND

This chapter introduces and explains the architecture of the Polymorphic Mind. It defines *Psychic Polymorphism*, showing you how we all operate from a constellation of sub-personalities ("Parts"). You will learn how we become fragmented and how that fragmentation is a survival advantage in early life that becomes a trap in adulthood. Most importantly, you will understand how your Authentic SELF—the quiet leader within you—can reclaim its rightful role. You'll come away with a map of your inner world and the first glimpse of the peace that lies on the other side of internal chaos.

You are not your brain.

That statement might feel strange, even disorienting. After all, we've been taught to equate our thoughts with our identity. We've learned to say things like "I think, therefore I am" and to treat every mental whisper as a reflection of our most authentic self. But here's the truth: You are not your brain. It is a remarkable tool, but it is not the whole of you. It is part of the stage crew, not the playwright.

Understanding this distinction is essential because, if we believe we *are* our brain, we become enslaved to its chatter. We take every thought as gospel, every fear as prophecy, and every judgment as fact. But the brain is not designed to tell us the truth about who we are. It is only designed to keep us alive.

In this way, your brain is more like a highly sophisticated survival machine than a source of wisdom. It scans for danger, recalls pain, and rehearses worst-case scenarios. It overemphasizes threats and underestimates your strengths. And it does not automatically update itself with your growing maturity or capacity.

Despite your very real adult accomplishments, your brain often still sees you through the lens of your earliest vulnerabilities. It speaks to you as if you're still the frightened child who needed to please, perform, or disappear to stay safe. And because this neurological architecture forms early and powerfully, it can shape your internal world for decades, even after your external world has dramatically changed. In short,

The brain fails to recalibrate as we grow up.

Instead of recognizing your evolution, it continues to run neural algorithms developed to protect a small, powerless child. These outdated patterns—the ego constructs that I call Parts or sub-personalities—are not signs of weakness. They are the very strategies that got you safely to adulthood. But now, they are trying to drive a life they were never meant to lead.

And because you are not your brain, you are invited to step back. You have the opportunity to become a powerful observer.

From the seat of your true SELF, we'll begin a journey—not just through neuroscience and psychology but into the inner design of your mind. From that grounded vantage point, everything changes.

In the pages ahead, we'll explore what it means to live from your true SELF. We'll examine the architecture of your mind using the *Polymorphic Mind Model (PMM)*, and we'll look at how you can begin to reestablish internal leadership in a way that honors your full story without being trapped by it.

As we advance, it is critical for you to remember this:

You are not your brain.

You are something far more extraordinary. Let's discover what that is.

IN THE BEGINNING

I have traveled and worked among some of the most vulnerable, disadvantaged children in the world. And I have observed a surprising characteristic that seems to radiate from children in even the most dangerous and downtrodden circumstances: their happiness.

Children appear to be born fundamentally happy. Actually, they are more than happy. They are also kind, curious, confident, generous, and connected. They exhibit an intrinsic sense of trust and wonder, effortlessly engaging with the world and those around them.

So it appears that, at birth, every one of us embodies a singular, integrated essence characterized by our very best innate qualities. This untainted, original self—which

I call the Authentic SELF—enters the world full of purity, positivity, and potential, unburdened by fear, self-doubt, or the need for protection.

It is as though we enter this life in a state of psychological perfection—not in the sense of flawlessness but in an inherent wholeness and completeness that requires nothing more to be fully realized.

A newborn does not question their worth, nor do they seek external validation to justify their existence. Instead, they move through the world with undiluted joy and openness, embracing life with an absence of judgment, shame, and self-restriction. Their Authentic SELF sees and feels without distortion, allowing for deep engagement with the present moment.

But that's not where the story ends, though, because we are also born useless.

We are, in fact, born perfectly useless.

Unlike other advanced mammals that enter the world equipped to fend for themselves, human infants arrive in a state of profound dependency, requiring years of support and protection before they become self-sufficient.

Fascinatingly, our profound helplessness at birth is directly tied to the extraordinary nature of the human brain. The human brain is magnificently complex and disproportionately large at maturity—so much so that the fully developed human brain far exceeds the dimensions of the narrow pelvic canal through which it must pass at birth. This forces an evolutionary compromise: Unlike many other species, which are born with brains nearly fully developed for immediate survival, we are born neurologically premature. In essence, we enter the world long before our brains reach functional maturity, making us uniquely dependent on external care and guidance for survival.

THE ENTRENCHMENT OF UNIQUE COMPLEXITY

To bridge the gap between helplessness and competence, Nature imposes a rigorous developmental trajectory, forcefully stretching individuals toward maturity.

When we are born, we are estimated to have between 80 and 100 billion individual nerve cells (called *neurons*) in our brain.[7] We know that every neuron connects to many other neurons, each playing their own unique role in the computational circuit that is formed. Within this staggering lattice of connectivity, it is estimated that we have over 100 trillion connections,[8] each contributing to our own distinct neurobiological complexion.

For the first two years of our life, the brain is connecting these neurons at a voracious pace. Scientists believe that over a million connections are made per second during this period.[9] This leaves us with incomprehensibly vast computational capability by the age of two. And then, a very interesting thing happens. To limit the unsupportable energy demands of such a huge biological supercomputer, to facilitate reasonable mental focus, and to adapt to our particular context, we start breaking down the less-useful connections.[10]

This process leaves us with collections of nerves that wire and work together to enable survival in our own unique context. It is also this process that results in our individual personality. Different from all the other 8 billion living human beings, we each have our own unique "psychic fingerprint," thanks to our unique neurological growth journey.

The process of adaptive neurobiological specialization ensures that we emerge as a heterogeneous mosaic of sub-personalities, each shaped by specific experiences, stressors, and survival demands. Every significant emotional challenge, particularly in early life, reinforces and refines distinct neural circuits, strengthening the dominance of certain protective Parts over time. As a result, rather than a singular identity, we form a network of semiautonomous sub-personalities designed to address past threats, each with its own behavioral patterns, emotional reactivities, and cognitive biases. These Parts, while essential for navigating a complex world, eventually create a heterogenous, survival-oriented mask—the "false self"—composed of fragmented sub-personalities that distance us from the effortless joy, trust, and completeness we once knew.

It's this essential understanding that underpins Psychic Polymorphism: In response to the relentless stretches of neural development, the brain adapts by constructing protective algorithms, psychological mechanisms designed to ensure survival.

INTERNAL FRAGMENTATION

Each of our Parts is a distinct neural pattern governing thought, emotion, and behavior. It is this collection of sub-personalities that forms who we are and gives rise to my term *Psychic Polymorphism*. The word "poly" means many, and the word "morph" means shape. So, our mind is formed by the aggregation of many shapes (or sub-personalities).

Depending on which algorithm is dominant at a given moment, we may appear to embody entirely different personalities, a stark departure from the magnificent wholeness of our newborn selves and a direct expression of the survival strategies etched into our mind over time. When triggered, each Part reacts to produce a predictable and distinct attitudinal and behavioral projection that is often at odds with our essence. Little Daniel, who once learned to earn affection through achievement, later found himself compulsively striving in adult boardrooms—chasing success not from a calm place of clear vision but from a deep-seated fear of being unseen.

Over time, these neural patterns become deeply ingrained, often surfacing reflexively in response to triggers and bypassing conscious decision-making. With repeated use, the neural pathways governing these sub-personalities strengthen (or *hypertrophy*), much like deepened grooves in a well-worn path. A key consequence of nerve hypertrophy is the increased speed of activation in neural pathways.[11] Unlike muscles, which grow stronger with repeated use, nerves become *faster* with repeated use. This acceleration is due to the thickening of the myelin sheath— the insulating layer surrounding nerve fibers—which physiologically enhances conduction speed.[12]

As a result, frequently triggered protective algorithms fire with reflexive immediacy, outpacing any alternative responses that require more deliberation. These deeply ingrained survival mechanisms engage faster than we can consciously think, an adaptive advantage for a vulnerable child but a profound limitation for a competent adult.

What once ensured our safety now precludes our choice, trapping us in automatic reactions. These deeply ingrained Parts often operate anachronistically, responding to present circumstances with outdated strategies that no longer serve our best interests. What began as an elegant survival mechanism now manifests as internal conflict, a battle between our Authentic SELF and the collection of protective constructs that have taken the reins of our behavior.

Moreover, these sub-personalities often employ conflicting strategies, further intensifying our inner discord. One Part may instinctively urge flight and another may demand complete withdrawal and invisibility, while yet another may default to aggression and attack. This contradiction in protective impulses leaves us oscillating between incompatible responses, compounding stress and reinforcing a sense of internal fragmentation rather than cohesion.

THE NATURE OF PROTECTIVE PARTS

Each Part, no matter how polished or persuasive, is ultimately driven by fear.

Beneath its surface behavior lies a single mission: to protect you from perceived threat—not necessarily physical danger but, more often, emotional and psychological perils like rejection, shame, failure, and abandonment.

To protect you, each Part adopts a fear-driven action, what I refer to in the PMM as one of the "Seven Fs." These are ancient survival patterns, coded into your nervous system and deployed reflexively.

This poetic structure may help you to remember the seven safety-first survival imperatives that govern your sub-personalities:

> *They **fight**, take **flight**, or **freeze** in fear;*
> *They **fawn** to please or **frame** what's near.*
> *They **fix** what's wrong or **feign** I'm fine—*
> *All ways they guard this heart of mine.*

Each Part is a servant loyal to one of these strategies, doing whatever it must to keep you safe and translating ancient biological impulses into modern emotional patterns.

You may recognize where each of these primal instincts appears in our story:

- Fight (confront to gain control): Olga channels her disciplined stoicism into relentless achievement, vigorously confronting every challenge with intensity to maintain control over her emotions and environment.

- Flight (escape to avoid pain): Daniel overachieves obsessively, fleeing any sense of unworthiness by constructing an impeccable life of success behind which he can hide.

- Freeze (immobilize to become invisible): Sora retreats into elegant silence, cloaking herself in aesthetic ideals and refined cultural trappings. Her grace is disarming, an artful veil that conceals her deepest longings and shields her from emotional exposure.

- Fawn (please to stay safe): Awa perfects every aspect of her persona to elicit praise and avoid disapproval, using excellence as a shield to please those whose love feels conditional.

- Frame (intellectualize to avoid perceived danger): Alexei dissociates emotionally, freezing into hyperrational analysis whenever feelings threaten to break through his controlled façade.

- Fix (solve to reduce tension): Liam habitually steps in to mediate or lift the emotional weight of others, fixing problems to avoid his own buried exhaustion and need for care.

- Feign (perform to maintain belonging): Rafael plays the role of impassioned leader, projecting certainty and nurturing charisma to ensure he's never left behind again, even when he feels unsure or alone inside.

Though their strategies differ, these Parts' origin is the same: a deep, often unconscious belief that the world is not safe and that your survival depends on their unyielding control.

Their expression can range from a quiet, almost imperceptible influence—like the soft insistence of a People Pleaser gently taking the wheel to steer you toward approval and away from conflict—to dramatic, even reckless activism, as seen in the frenzied grip of a Desperate Escapist that turns to alcohol or drugs in an attempt to avoid unbearable inner turmoil.

Understanding these fear-based missions allows us to see our Parts not as problems to be eliminated but as outdated guardians in need of compassionate reassignment.

THE SHADOWS: TRAGIC MEMORIES

At the core of every protective sub-personality lies a shadow memory—a charged trace of trauma, neglect, shame, or loss. These memories exist as conscious electrophysiological imprints in the brain, shaping your ongoing responses to life. Though they live in the past, they function in the present, silently directing much of your internal world. They are encoded with intensity, are stored deep in the nervous system, and often surface not as thoughts but as physical sensations, emotional surges, or reflexive behaviors that seem disproportionate or puzzling.

Neurologically, painful or traumatic memories are encoded differently than neutral or positive experiences. The *amygdala*, the brain's emotional alarm system, flags distressing events with urgency, prioritizing them for survival.[13] Meanwhile, the *hippocampus*, which normally tags memories with context and time, often under-functions in the midst of trauma.[14] This impairment means these memories are not properly filed away; they remain raw, vivid, and timeless. The result? They don't feel like memories. They feel like *now*.

This classification system makes perfect sense for a helpless child who must survive real danger. But for the competent adult you've become, it creates a painful mismatch: ancient alarms still blaring in a world you've already mastered.

When triggered, the body doesn't simply remember. It reenacts. The nervous system reacts as if the original event is reoccurring, flooding you with emotion, tension, or fear that has no obvious cause.[15]

Over time, these imprints become the birthplaces of protective sub-personalities— the internal protectors whose sole mission is to prevent the wound from being touched again. They adopt whatever strategy is necessary: withdrawal, perfectionism, aggression, addiction, charm. They operate with fierce loyalty and frozen logic, reacting as if the danger is ongoing.

Because these Parts are guarding a wound that feels active and unhealed, they are deeply suspicious of change. Healing feels like risk. Growth feels like exposure. This is why we often sabotage our progress, repeat old patterns, or resist transformation— even when we know better. It is because...

The false self is designed not for happiness but for protection.

Not all distressing experiences lead to equally powerful memories. The brain tends to encode repeated, developmentally significant, or high-intensity experiences with greater permanence.[16] Key factors influencing the strength of a shadow memory include age, emotional intensity, and reinforcement.[17]

Earlier trauma leaves a deeper neurological imprint, as the brain is still forming core identity structures.[18] Additionally, the greater the distress, the stronger the encoding. Moments of shame, abandonment, powerlessness, or terror often create the most dominant shadow memories.[19]

And finally, if a distressing experience recurs (e.g., chronic criticism or ongoing neglect), the shadow memory becomes even more deeply ingrained, reinforcing the Part that was created to protect against it.[20] When young Daniel's small triumphs were routinely met with indifference—a nod, silence, a glance that moved on—the Part of him that longed for recognition began choreographing exceptional performances, each one a desperate bid for applause loud enough to silence the ache of being unseen.

THE DESIGN FLAW

By now, I am sure that you have recognized that the PMM reveals what I describe as an inherent design flaw in the development of the human psyche: While our external world evolves and our mental competence expands, the survival-based sub-personalities within us remain frozen in time. This unchanging internal architecture creates a cascade of challenges in adulthood, barriers that must be consciously addressed to regain full psychological freedom.

The root of the problem is that our brain doesn't notice that we've grown up. As a result, it continues deploying the same protective strategies it used in childhood, even in adult situations where they are maladaptive. The problem is not that these strategies have no value but that they persist long after we have outgrown them.

For instance, as a child, running and hiding may have been the best option to avoid an abusive or chaotic situation. Swinging fists may have been necessary to defend oneself against playground bullies. People pleasing may have been a survival mechanism for securing safety and approval from caregivers.

As a competent adult, you now have access to better tools—conflict resolution, emotional intelligence, negotiation, and self-advocacy—yet these outdated protective Parts still react as if you were a helpless child. It is no longer appropriate to shut down emotionally, lash out in anger, or compulsively seek approval, yet these old behaviors still surface before you have a chance to choose differently.

The brain doesn't automatically update these survival strategies to match our adult capabilities; it clings to what once worked, assuming we are still as vulnerable as we were when these Parts first emerged.

Three Dilemmas

To overcome this neurological design flaw, we must first confront three dilemmas.

The first is a dilemma of enslavement, which lies in how we are biologically and socially conditioned to grant our brain unquestioned authority from the very beginning of life.

As we've already noted, humans arrive in the world profoundly helpless. A baby must rely entirely on others for months, even years. As a result, the helpless human child is taught to obey its brain unquestioningly. This obedience is necessary for survival in childhood; in the context of early life, it makes perfect sense to treat every signal from the brain as vital: every fear as urgent and every strategy as sacred. But this deference becomes dangerous when we forget to update it.

As we mature, we fail to recognize that we have outgrown the need for blind submission. The brain's protective mechanisms don't evolve automatically just because we do. They continue issuing orders based on an old internal biography—a version of us that no longer exists.

Thus, we remain obedient to our brain, following outdated neural instructions as if they were absolute truth rather than recognizing the brain as a tool meant to serve us. Until we pause, examine, and update that inherited loyalty, we remain ruled by a mind that is trying to save someone we no longer are.

The next dilemma to confront is one of identification. One of the most insidious effects of survival-driven sub-personalities is their ability to merge seamlessly into our inner narrative, masquerading as our true identity. Because these Parts arise early and stay active for decades, they begin to feel familiar, like longtime friends or internal advisors whose voices have always been with us.

Over time, we stop seeing them as distinct. Their messages—once protective—are adopted wholesale as self-truths. Instead of recognizing them as adaptive responses to early adversity, we identify with them entirely: "I'm just an anxious person," or "I've always been a perfectionist," or "I can't handle conflict," or "I need to be heard."

The truth is that these *aren't* statements of identity. They are declarations of surreptitious alliance with specific Parts, echoes of internal figures still trying to protect us from long-past pain. But, because they sound like our own thoughts, we rarely question them.

This mistaken identification is reinforced by a psychological process known as *individuation*.[21] As we grow, we naturally begin to form a sense of self. The first voices we hear in our heads as we separate from our parents are these protective algorithms. We look around to see who has spoken, but, of course, there is nobody there. So we assume the voices must be our own. We mistake their vigilance for wisdom and their rigidity for strength.

And so, we build a self-concept around them. The Part becomes not just an advisor but the narrator. Not just *a* voice but *the* voice. This is the identification dilemma:

The false self doesn't *feel* false.

It feels familiar, even essential. And until we step back and begin to witness these Parts from the seat of our Authentic SELF, we will continue to live their stories—no matter how outdated, limiting, or painful they've become.

The final dilemma facing us is one of speed. You will remember that, at the heart of this design flaw, there is one fundamental reality: In the brain, speed dominates. Sub-personalities dictate behavior because they react faster than we can think.

You'll recall that neurons grow faster with repeated use.[22] As a result, the most frequently triggered protective algorithms fire with reflexive immediacy, vastly outpacing alternative responses that require conscious thought.

This design is brilliant for a child, where split-second survival decisions—fight, flee, freeze, fawn, frame, fix, or feign—must override rational processing. But for an adult with complex cognitive and emotional resources, this same design becomes a limitation rather than an advantage. It ensures that we react rather than respond, automatically repeating outdated, maladaptive survival strategies before we have a chance to deliberately select a better approach.

THE PROBLEM WITH GROWING UP

The many consequences of the human design flaw must be coming clear to you now. But two dramatic issues stand out for me more than the rest.

The first is that the chaotic inner chorus that is born to save us dis-integrates us, creating conflict and confusion.

Each Part has a voice and a vote—which, while creating adaptability and diversity, can also lead to overwhelming inner noise and confusion. This is why reintegration becomes the fundamental objective of our work; the goal is not to silence the fragmented Parts but to restore authority to the Authentic SELF.

In my experience, though, the greatest issue by far with our human design is that it makes inevitable a psychological phenomenon that has now emerged as a florid reality we all face, based simply on our common design: imposter syndrome.

Imposter syndrome isn't a flaw; it's a consequence of growing up.

This is the distortion the PMM reveals most clearly: the chronic, internal misidentification that leaves capable adults feeling small, fragile, and unworthy, regardless of their external accomplishments.

At the heart of this distortion lies a tragic and nearly invisible truth: The brain continues to treat us as if we were still children. And because our protective Parts were formed to guide, control, and defend a vulnerable child, they never update their tone. They continue to speak with the same patronizing, fearful, belittling voices they once used to control and protect our helpless young self.

This is the hidden engine of imposter syndrome.

We don't just *feel* like we're not enough—we're *told* so, again and again, by voices inside our mind that we mistake for our own. These voices of Parts that think they're protecting us are actually reinforcing the very self-doubt they were built to defend against.

This creates what I call the "self-belittling cycle," a self-reinforcing loop that binds even the most accomplished adults in invisible chains.

This cycle often begins innocently enough. A Part is activated, perhaps in response to stress, a new challenge, or even a subtle perceived threat. Without conscious awareness, it steps forward, delivering its internal monologue in familiar tones of anxiety, criticism, perfectionism, or shame. Though the voice sounds like your own, it's actually echoing a much older story, one rooted in early vulnerability and fear.

The adult self, unaware of the origin, reacts instinctively. A wave of inadequacy washes in—feelings of fraudulence, incompetence, or insecurity—often accompanied by suboptimal choices or diminished performance. And because those reactions reinforce the sense of deficiency, the person doubles down on their Parts: more control, more performing, more hiding, more striving.

This, of course, validates the original Part's role, deepening the neural grooves of the pattern. The loop tightens. The mind begins to trust the familiar discomfort of self-doubt over the unfamiliar freedom of authenticity.

And with each repetition, the voice of the Part becomes more convincing and the voice of the Authentic SELF becomes harder to hear.

This loop becomes self-perpetuating. Even as our lives grow, our self-concept remains stunted. The tragedy is not that we are incapable; it's that we are unable to experience our capability. We simply don't know how capable we are because, no matter how much we achieve, we still feel like a child playing dress-up in adult clothes.

Here's how this pattern often plays out in the real world:

A Perfectionist Part quietly steps forward and whispers, "You're only valuable if you do this flawlessly." It feels like motivation, but it's really pressure disguised as worth. You respond as you always have: pushing harder, sacrificing rest, chasing control. There's no room for error, only performance.

And then, inevitably, you falter, not because you're not capable but because perfection is impossible. And in your moment of struggle, that same voice turns cold: "See? I told you. You're not really good enough. You're a fraud."

The shame lands hard. You don't pause to question the source. Instead, you double down: more striving, more fixing, more pressure. The cycle continues. The suffering deepens. And all the while, your Authentic SELF—the part of you that doesn't need to prove, perform, or perfect—remains hidden beneath layers of armor.

This is not weakness. It is misalignment. And it is nearly universal.

The truth is, discovering you have imposter syndrome isn't proof that you don't belong; it's proof that a Part of you hasn't yet realized that you do.

A Haunting, Hidden Script

There's something subtle, almost imperceptible, that happens when a Part speaks.

You won't hear it out loud. You may not even register it consciously. But if you listen carefully—if you slow down the internal dialogue just enough—you'll notice that nearly every protective message begins the same way: "Hey, little boy..." or "Hey, little girl..."

Of course, the words themselves are never spoken. They're encoded, tucked into the tone, the timing, and the posture of the thought. But they're always there, a whispered preface that locates you not in your present strength but in your past fragility. Before the critique, the panic, and the drive to fix, please, or perfect comes this silent invocation of your smallest self.

It's how a successful executive can feel like a fraud after one mistake.

It's how a world-class athlete can be reduced to tears by a single glance.

It's how we—grown, capable, even admired—can feel utterly unworthy without understanding why.

Because beneath the words we consciously hear—"You're not good enough..." "You always mess this up..." "You'd better get this right..."—there is that whispered invocation: *Hey, little one...you're still not safe.*

This is the heart of imposter syndrome. It is not a flaw in your character but a flaw in your brain's calibration. It is not a lack of success but a legacy of mistaken identity, where the voices that were once designed to protect a helpless child are now misfiring in the life of a powerful adult.

And unless we hear that opening line—unless we recognize who the message is truly meant for—we'll keep mistaking it as truth.

But once we do hear it, *really* hear it, we can respond not as the frightened child but as the calm, clear, compassionate SELF.

And that changes everything.

Fortunately, as you'll see in the next chapter, there is a path forward. By recognizing this pattern, engaging it with compassion, and reconnecting with the integrated wisdom of your Authentic SELF, you can finally step out of the loop.

You can silence the belittling echoes of the past.

And you can begin to live in the full magnitude of your original and enduring truth.

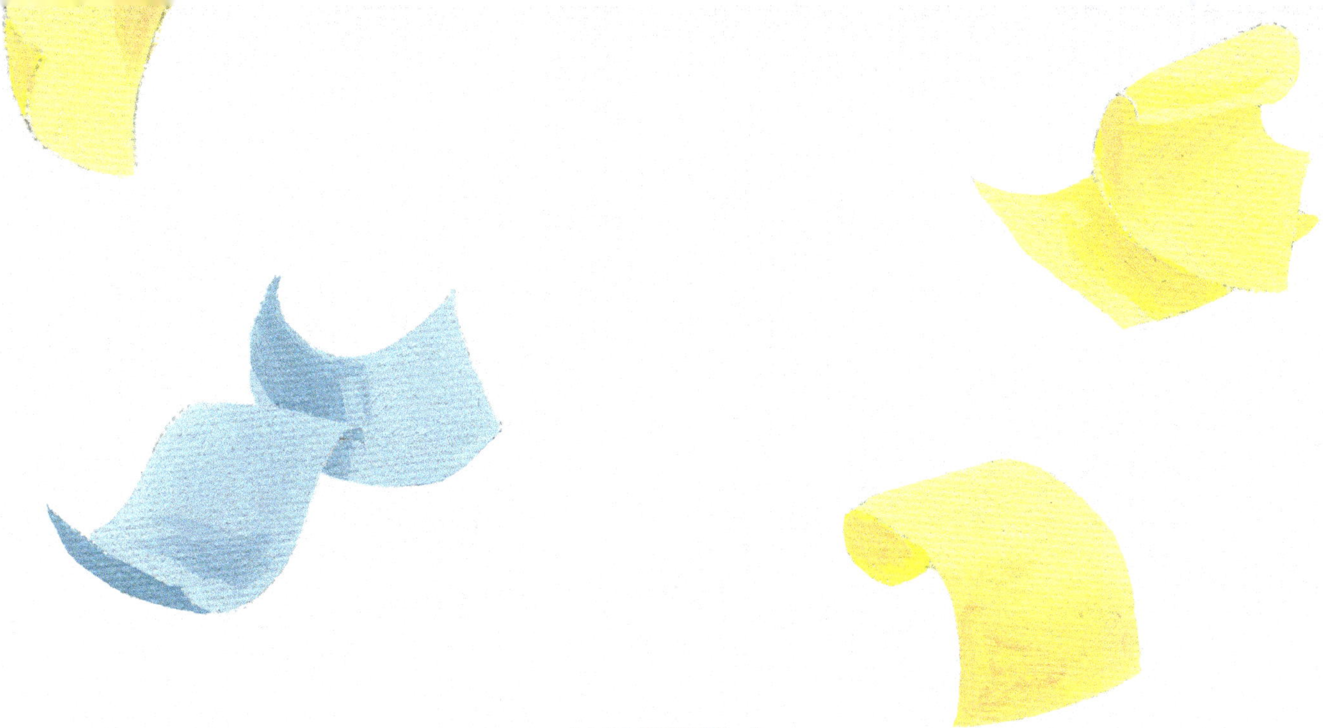

CHAPTER 4

The Path to Authentic SELF

Understanding the structure of your mind is only the beginning. Now that you recognize the cast of Parts that have been running the show, the real question becomes this: Who should lead? In this chapter, we'll explore how to invite your Authentic SELF to take the director's seat, not with force but with compassion, clarity, and confidence. Transformation begins when you inhabit your mind differently, so we'll review the stages of reintegration, preparing you for your journey back to your SELF.

You've made it this far—through the tangle of borrowed identities, protective masks, and well-worn survival scripts. You've explored the architecture of your mind, uncovered the source of your fragmentation, and named the silent dilemma that shapes adult suffering. You now stand on the edge of something new.

Up to this point, we've been laying the groundwork for understanding the problem with growing up. But knowledge alone cannot heal. Understanding how the mind is shaped by Parts—those sub-personalities forged in moments of stress and survival— is essential, but insufficient. Something more is needed now: action. Transformation.

Here begins the shift from knowing to changing, from insight to embodiment, and from Parts-led reactivity to SELF-led reintegration.

If the previous chapters were the map, this chapter is your compass and plan. It offers a practical, proven, and compassionate process to navigate the path home to your true nature. Here, we begin the core transformational journey: how we evolve from being unconsciously led by Parts to being consciously led by the Authentic SELF.

The work ahead is not about exiling or silencing your Parts. They are not enemies to be conquered. They are loyal, albeit sometimes misguided, protectors. You will learn to engage them with kindness and curiosity. You will learn to listen, and to lead.

This chapter will guide you through a clear arc, from the first flicker of self-awareness to recognizing the signs of out-of-control sub-personalities, and into the theatre of your imagination where inner dialogue and healing begin. You'll discover how to identify which Part is active, how to gently bring compassion to its purpose, and how to reclaim authority with grace.

I call this *conscious reclamation*: the inner work that leads to outer peace. This is how we reclaim clarity, confidence, and calm. This is how we move from fragmentation to wholeness.

The journey begins now.

THE SEVEN STAGES OF REINTEGRATION

Until now, you've likely been led by your Parts without even realizing it. The voices of your Inner Critic, Anxious Planner, Charming Pleaser, and Furious Defender speak so fluently, so convincingly, that you mistake them for *you*. But they are not you. They are fragments, created to keep you safe when you were too small to survive alone.

They were brilliant, once. They got you through. But now, in adulthood, their leadership has become a liability. After all, Parts are survival specialists, not visionaries.

Your job is to reclaim leadership from your Parts and return it to your Authentic SELF. In effect, you will be putting the wise, compassionate presence of your SELF at the head of the table. When led by the SELF, your Parts can relax. They can advise, support, and contribute. And they can stop being in charge.

When you learn to hear them clearly—not as your identity but as signals—you begin to heal. You stop reacting. You start responding. You stop spiraling. You start choosing.

The path from suffering to sovereignty follows a series of developmental thresholds. This arc maps your movement from automatic reactivity to integrated presence, from a life led by protective algorithms to one guided by your Authentic SELF.

Stage One: Ignorance: You are led by Parts without awareness. Sub-personalities operate beneath the surface, below your conscious awareness. Their voices feel like your own. Reaction is automatic. Life feels driven by urgency, conflict, or emotional overwhelm. Suffering is familiar, and strangely normalized. There is no separation between you and the systems that govern you.

Stage Two: Recognition: Something shifts. You catch yourself, eventually, in the act—snapping at a loved one, withdrawing in fear, spiraling into perfectionism—and instead of merging with it, you notice it. "Something in me is afraid," you say. Not, "I am afraid." This is the moment you create the tiniest space between stimulus and response, and in that space, freedom begins to grow. The Part is still active, but now you see it. And seeing it changes everything.

Stage Three: Exploration: You turn toward the Part with curiosity, not judgment. What does this Part want? What is it protecting? When did it first appear? How has it helped you? You resist the impulse to fix, suppress, or analyze. Instead, you listen. You begin to map its story and function. This is not about explaining the Part away; it's about building a relationship with it.

Stage Four: Understanding: The Part becomes more than a behavior or a burden. You understand its intention: to protect. You understand its origin: a moment when your safety—emotional or physical—felt threatened. And you understand its cost: limits to your growth. Compassion deepens. Blame fades. The Part becomes less of a problem and more of a messenger.

Stage Five: Disentanglement: You are no longer fused with the Part. It still arises, but you no longer collapse into it. You hear its voice, but you don't obey its commands. You feel its urgency, but you respond with stillness. This is not detachment or denial; it is differentiation. You now have space to choose.

Stage Six: Authority: With practice, your Authentic SELF reclaims leadership. The Part is no longer driving. It may speak, but it no longer steers. It may signal, but it no longer decides. It returns to its appropriate place: as an advisor in the inner room, but not the one holding the steering wheel of your life. You lead from clarity, not fear. Calm, not compulsion. The system begins to reorder itself around your SELF.

Stage Seven: Reintegration: Eventually, what once required conscious effort becomes natural again. The Part's reactive pattern—once automatic—has been downregulated and repatterned. You no longer need to manage it moment by moment. The Part becomes a contributor to the whole, not a hijacker. There is harmony without hypervigilance. The nervous system rests. The mind quiets. The SELF's leadership becomes less effortful and more instinctual.

This is not abstract theory. It's real. It plays out in the heated moments of a meeting, the heartbreak of a relationship, and the doubt that keeps you awake at night. In each moment, you can choose. You can notice. You can pause. And with practice, you can shift from being hijacked by a protective Part to being guided by the calm clarity of your SELF.

From here, we begin the journey inward—into the arena, where Parts show up and the work begins.

RECOGNIZING AN ACTIVE PART

The journey of transformation begins with recognition. To reclaim authority from your Parts, you must first learn to notice when one has taken the lead.

Often, Parts announce themselves through intensity. You might feel a sudden emotional spike: rage that seems disproportionate, fear that arrives without clear cause, or shame that tightens your chest like a vice. Or perhaps the signal is subtler: a loop of thoughts you can't shake, a self-critical script on repeat, or a need to flee or freeze that overtakes you before you've had time to consider your options. These are the telltale signs of a Part in control.

The signs are often physiological as well. One of my favorite clients came to me simply because she couldn't relax her clenched jaw.

For you, it might be a racing heart. Shallow breath. A collapsing posture. Facial muscles that harden without consent. These cues, though often dismissed as stress or fatigue, are the somatic language of sub-personalities asserting control.

As an advanced practitioner of this method myself, I've found that the most reliable indicator that a Part is active in me is this: I simply don't feel good. A shift in mood or a sense of unease, frustration, or internal pressure: These are often the fingerprints of a deeply embedded algorithm surfacing in response to some perceived threat. Over time, I've learned to treat every negative emotional state as a gentle nudge to pause and look inward.

There are a few simple but powerful internal tests to help you become aware of your Parts. The voice test asks, *Does the voice in my head sound extreme, absolute, or accusatory?* Parts sometimes speak in black-and-white terms. They lack nuance, empathy, and balance. The urgency test prompts, *Does this experience feel pressured or rushed?* Parts often demand immediate action. They push for reaction, not reflection. And the fusion test wonders, *Am I consumed by this state?* When a

Part is fully blended with your consciousness, it feels like the whole truth. There's no room for perspective. No witness remains. It's not "a part of me is angry"; it's "*I am angry*." You might find it difficult to come up with alternative explanations when in the grip of a Part.

Beneath these experiences lies a neurological reality. When a Part hijacks your system, the more primitive regions of your brain—the survival circuits—come online, often bypassing the slower, wiser regions of your prefrontal cortex. This is not a flaw. It's biology. Your brain, once again, is trying to keep you safe using outdated rules. But what helped you survive at age five may no longer serve you at 45.

For most of us, the instinct is to suppress or outthink these inner voices—to push them away, fix them, or dismiss them as irrational. But true transformation doesn't begin with force. It begins with dialogue. And to have that dialogue, we need a space, a setting where these invisible characters can safely reveal themselves, be heard, and begin to evolve.

The first skill, then, is not to suppress the Part or shame it away. It is to notice. To pause. To say inwardly, "Something in me is activated," and allow a breath of space to open between you and the reaction. In that space, your observations grow stronger. Awareness is progress. Recognition is power.

Recognizing a Part in motion is the first step toward healing.

Now that you've begun to notice your Parts, the question becomes this: What do you do with them?

WELCOME TO THE THEATRE OF YOUR IMAGINATION

To answer that question, let's move into the theatre of your imagination. This theatre is a method. It's a practical, powerful, and deeply humane tool that allows you to witness your inner world with clarity and compassion. Here, in the privacy of your mind, you can invite your Parts to take shape. You can see them, speak with them, and listen to what they need. You can give them a seat at the table—but, crucially, under your leadership.

One of the most impactful insights on my personal journey was realizing that our thoughts, behaviors, and emotional patterns are driven by deep neural algorithms, real code etched into the brain through experience. But because we can't read or reach this code directly, we need a translator. I found that stories—personal, symbolic, and imagined—could serve as that bridge. By entering the theatre of the imagination, I could uncover the histories shaping these algorithms and begin to redraft them. The results were profound. The more I used this method—with myself and with my clients—the more powerful the transformation. In time, I understood: We have access to the programs that govern us; through the language of story, we can begin to rewrite the underlying code that makes us who we are.

This approach is further supported by the science. By engaging your prefrontal cortex, you can release your imaginative executive functions to do magical work. When you imagine, you activate a part of your brain known as the *default mode network (DMN)*.[23] This network enables self-referential thinking and autobiographical processing. It's also the seat of your brain's natural storytelling capacity. By visualizing your Parts—giving them names, faces, postures, and voices—you create distance without disconnection. You transform chaotic inner noise into coherent inner conversation.

The heart of the practice is reintegration. You're not dissecting your Parts to fix them; you're meeting them with respectful curiosity. You're becoming the wise adult leader these Parts have always longed for.

Creatively, the theatre invites safety. You don't need to be accurate, only honest. You might see your Inner Critic as a stern schoolteacher. Your Anxious Planner might appear as a clipboard-wielding project manager. Your Heavy Rager might take the shape of an exhausted parent. These images are not diagnoses. They are doors, pathways to connection.

Some people picture their Parts sitting around a boardroom table. Others stage the theatre on a quiet forest path or in an inner temple. There's no correct setting. What matters is presence, openness, and the willingness to see what appears when you ask, "Who's here right now?"

This practice may feel strange at first. That's natural. Imagination has been wrongly relegated to childhood or fantasy. But in truth, it's one of your brain's most sophisticated tools for healing. Used skillfully, it becomes a space of safety, insight, and transformation.

So don't worry if it feels awkward or artificial to begin with. Trust the process. Keep showing up. Over time, your Parts will begin to trust you, too.

You're not fabricating your inner world—you're finally listening to it.

DIRECTING THE DRAMA: CONSCIOUS RECLAMATION

Now that you've begun to recognize your Parts and entered the theatre of your imagination, your path to transformation is ready to unfold. This next section is your practical guide to healing—a return to the transformational arc, now lived in the actions of conscious reclamation.

Begin by moving from Ignorance to Recognition. You begin by noticing. This may be retrospective at first, after the outburst or the withdrawal. But even delayed recognition matters. "I didn't feel like myself," becomes, "Something in me was afraid." The moment you shift from "*I* am angry" to "*A part of me* is angry," you have moved from fusion to awareness. The arc has begun.

Move from Recognition to Exploration. With the Part now visible, your task is to explore with gentle curiosity. What is this Part trying to protect? What memory or fear is it harboring? What does it want you to avoid? Ask, "What do I feel right now?" and then, "Who might be feeling this?" In the moment, remember: A Part reacts, but the true SELF responds. Listen for the first voice to know who is speaking. This is the turning point from judgment to inquiry and from rejection to rapport.

Move from Exploration to Understanding. Now you begin to know the Part, not just *what* it does but *why*. You see its protective function, perhaps once life-saving but now misfiring. You glimpse the wound behind the wall. You don't excuse its behavior, but you understand its origin. This is where compassion is born: deep recognition of what the Part has endured and why it still fights. Appreciation for its efforts begins to take root in you.

Move from Understanding to Disentanglement. You create space. You begin to feel the Part's energy without being consumed by it. You hear its voice without obeying it. This isn't distance born of disconnection; it's the clarity that comes from perspective. You are not the angry voice. You are not the panicked planner. You are not the relentless performer. You are the one who can witness, appreciate, and guide them. This shift—simple but profound—is the core of inner sovereignty.

Move from Disentanglement to Authority. This is where SELF steps forward, a calm, grounded leader who brings coherence to the inner table. SELF-leadership is not built on domination. It emerges through presence, clarity, and relational trust. The Parts begin to sense this and slowly yield. They come to see that they no longer have to guard the gate. Someone wiser is home. Without their noticing it, you have grown into a fine, intelligent, and experienced adult. You are no longer the perfectly useless child. You begin to reorient your brain and its deep algorithms to the truth that you've got this.

This leadership flows not just from compassion and calm but from courage, creativity, grounded insight, intuitive knowing, fierce integrity, and soft wisdom. It looks like holding boundaries with kindness. It sounds like making decisions from inner alignment. It feels like agency, coherence, and dignity.

One of the simplest yet most powerful tools in stepping into authority is naming the Part. Neuroscience affirms what experience reveals: When we name them, we tame them.

When we give a Part a name—one that captures its tone, posture, and style—we bring it out of the shadows and into relationship.

In this work, I often use evocative, two-word names that blend descriptive tone with symbolic truth.

Names like the Desperate Performer, the Cold Stoic, or the Scheming Perfectionist illuminate a character. They help you recognize the Part when it shows up again, and they invite a sense of warmth and story rather than shame. As you listen to your Part's voice and energy, let the name arise from how it feels, what it wants, and what role it's playing. The right name will feel instantly familiar—like you've known this character all your life.

Finally, move from Authority to Reintegration. Now the system begins to shift. What once required conscious effort becomes easy. You find yourself responding with wisdom where once you reacted with fear. Your internal world quiets. The Parts still exist, but they're no longer scrambling for control. They are heard, held, and appropriately placed. They still have a voice and a vote, but the boardroom becomes a collaborative space instead of a battlefield. The Part is no longer the driver, but a respected advisor.

Patterns rewire. Algorithms soften. And because the Part no longer has to scream to be heard, your nervous system begins to rest. As these old, reactive patterns are triggered less frequently, the neural pathways that once fired with urgency begin to atrophy. Their signals weaken and their speed diminishes, because nerve thickness is directly related to conduction velocity. What was once a reflexive reaction begins to slow. And, in that pause, a window begins to open: a moment of clarity. It is a chance to notice, to reflect, and to choose a different response. You now have time to think of alternative paths forward, no longer trapped in the reflex but grounded in the wisdom of your Authentic SELF.

Reintegration is not the erasure of Parts but the return of harmony.

When a Part speaks up—often with urgency, certainty, or fear—it helps to have a reflexive inner response. If you'd like the simplest possible approach to regaining authority, then try these three sentences that both honor the Part and gently reclaim leadership:

"Thank you. Respectfully, you're wrong. I've got this."

With these three phrases, you acknowledge the Part's intent, you offer perspective from the SELF, and you reaffirm your role as the calm leader of your inner system. It's about reassuring the Part that someone wiser is now in charge.

It's important to remember that reintegration is not a final destination; it's a living, ongoing practice. Parts may reemerge, especially in times of stress or fatigue. This isn't failure; it's simply another invitation to lead. Each return is an opportunity to deepen your relationship with the Part, to respond with even more clarity and compassion. Over time, what once felt like a cacophony of competing soloists becomes more like a symphonic ensemble, distinct voices still present but guided by a steady conductor. And that conductor is you.

This, then, is the full path of conscious reclamation. The PMM is not just a map of your inner architecture; it is an invitation to lead yourself home. The work is not to destroy what has protected you but to transform the system by reclaiming its center. And that center is not fear, shame, or perfection. It is you—your Authentic SELF—whole, wise, and ready.

The Trigger as Teacher

By now, you've traveled far. You've seen the mosaic of your inner world, recognized the influence of your Parts, and begun to reclaim leadership through the steady presence of your Authentic SELF.

You already understand the journey from fragmentation to wholeness. Now the question becomes this: How do you live it in real time? What do you do when your system is activated, when a Part flares up at work, in love, or in conflict? You see, the real work happens in the wild, in the heat of everyday life, where real triggers pull old patterns to the surface and demand our attention.

Mastery doesn't come from avoiding pain. It comes from learning how to respond rather than react. It comes from choosing presence in the face of provocation.

So, in the next chapter, we'll explore how to meet with awareness and grace those moments when the heart races, the jaw tightens, or the mind spirals. We'll learn to recognize triggers not as problems to avoid but as sacred messengers, signals pointing us toward the Parts that still need our care. We'll walk through a practical framework to navigate these moments, exploring prompts and tools you can use to stay centered and sovereign, even when the world pulls you off course.

Above all, we'll learn how to meet the tough moments with enduring grace.

CHAPTER 5

The Practice of Presence

You now understand the problem with growing up and the theory behind solving it. But what are the practical steps to reintegrating? In this chapter, we'll look at how to turn theory into practice. You'll learn methods for applying the Polymorphic Mind Model in your day-to-day life to put your Authentic SELF fully in control.

We've explored the architecture of your inner world and uncovered the Parts that have quietly shaped your life. You've learned how to recognize them, relate to them, and reclaim your role as the leader of your internal system. But what happens in the moment when life presses in and you feel the heat rise?

You've seen the map. You've held the compass. Now, we begin the actual walk.

This chapter is your guide to applying the PMM in real time. When the email lands. When the meeting turns tense. When your partner withdraws. When the parenting moment is hard. When your heart races or your stomach sinks or your voice tightens. This is the moment the theory must become practice.

Here, you'll learn how to recognize emotional triggers as sacred signals, evidence that a Part has stepped forward to protect you. You'll be guided, step by step, through real-world scenarios that show how to respond with awareness rather than reflex. You'll discover how to meet your Parts in conversation, how to pause with kindness, and how to recenter in your Authentic SELF—even under pressure.

As you move through these pages, you'll find practices, prompts, and pathways for bringing this work off the page and into your life. One moment at a time, one breath at a time, you'll begin to see that personal transformation doesn't require escape from the world: It starts right in the heart of it.

Let's begin.

WHEN THE TRIGGER STRIKES

You're in a conversation when something shifts. A tone. A look. A moment of silence. Suddenly, your stomach tightens. Your jaw locks. Words tumble out that you didn't plan on saying. Or you shut down completely, retreating inward without even realizing it. Later, you wonder: *What happened to me?*

This is what we call a *trigger*. It's the moment a protective sub-personality steps in to take control.

These are the moments when you lose contact with your centered Authentic SELF. You stop responding and start reacting. Something else takes the reins. That something is usually a Part. And although its intention is to keep you safe, it often does so in ways that are no longer helpful: lashing out, withdrawing, pleasing, or performing.

This reaction is not a character flaw. It's a neurobiological reflex. When you're triggered, your body mobilizes for protection faster than your thinking brain can act. Your system shifts out of relational presence and into survival protocol. You misread intent. You say things you don't mean. You brace for impact.

The good news is that being triggered is not failure. It's information. It's the sound of an activated sub-personality calling out for attention. And, if you learn how to listen, it becomes your most powerful portal to healing and reintegration.

Treat these moments not as setbacks but as sacred entry points to SELF-leadership. Studying your triggers gives you direct access to your neuropsychobiology and the unique cast of sub-personalities that make up your internal world. Every trigger is a trailhead. Every reaction is an invitation to get curious.

What you're learning now is simple but transformative:

Parts react. SELF responds.

And every time you choose awareness over autopilot, you strengthen the neural and emotional pathways that bring you home to your SELF.

THE FIVE-STEP TRIGGER-BASED PROCESS

How do you stay present when a Part takes over?

These five steps form a simple, repeatable process you can use anytime you feel emotionally triggered. They are not about controlling your Parts but about shifting your relationship to them from fear and confusion to clarity and leadership.

You won't always do these steps perfectly, but that's not the goal. The goal is presence and progress.

Even a partial application—pausing for a breath, naming a feeling, or asking a question—can change the trajectory of a moment and rewire your inner architecture over time. These steps help build trust between you and the committee of Parts within you. They are the practice of compassionate SELF-leadership in action.

Step 1: Pause: Interrupt the autopilot to open a window of awareness. In the heat of a trigger, everything speeds up. Your body tightens. Your thoughts race. You move to defend or disappear before you've had time to choose.

This first step is not complicated. It's a moment. A breath. A sacred interruption. It may sound like this: "I'm feeling activated. I need a moment." Or, "This feels familiar. Let me take a breath."

You can also record your physical, emotional, and behavioral responses. Often, just noticing what's happening begins to dissolve its grip.

Step 2: Name It: Identify the Part that has stepped forward. The goal here is to create psychological distance with compassion. You are not trying to banish the Part; you're simply recognizing that it is not the whole of you. It is merely a voice, a protector, a familiar inner character who has temporarily taken the wheel.

Start here:

- "Something in me is afraid of being wrong."

- "A part of me feels panicked."

- "Who is speaking right now?"

Then, investigate further:

- What is this Part trying to protect?

- What is the emotional flavor: shame, fear, anger, panic?

- What is this Part's dominant trait?

- How does it behave: withdrawal, attack, performance, complicity?

- How does this contrast it with your core personality?

Look for patterns across past moments with similar feelings or behaviors. This will help you recognize when a particular Part has been active before.

Once you get to know this character, you can name it using a vivid, two-part naming convention. The preferred structure for naming Parts follows an evocative formula:

- An adjective capturing the *how* of the Part's behavior or emotional tone, and

- A noun naming the Part's *deliberate action, identity, or strategy.*

Examples include the Tireless People Pleaser, the Silent Rescuer, the Jittery Joker, and the Frantic Fixer (and we'll explore more of these characters, and in more detail, in the next chapter).

This gives each Part a colorful, precise, and emotionally resonant name, which enhances your ability to recognize, describe, and engage with it more skillfully—especially within the theatre of your imagination.

These names create clarity, not caricature. They allow you to meet your Parts with intimacy, intelligence, and diplomacy, rather than fear or fusion.

Step 3: Understand It: Get curious about the Part's deeper purpose. Each Part has its own survival logic. Understanding that logic—however outdated or unhelpful it may now be—is essential to healing.

This is where patterns become extremely helpful. Reflect on your responses and behaviors right now and in similar circumstances. Use your own insight, and ask others to help you by sharing their observations. Ponder, "In what other situations have I felt and behaved similarly?" Look for patterns that connect these instances to uncover the recurring role a sub-personality plays. Analyze the patterns to determine the fears, needs, or desires the sub-personality is trying to protect or fulfill.

Here are questions to guide your understanding:

- What does this Part *do* when it takes over? Fight? Perform? Shut down?

- What emotions arise with this Part: anger, panic, sadness? What might these feelings be protecting?

- What stories accompany this Part? "I always mess it up"? "They're going to leave me"? "I can't trust anyone"?

- What fear or unmet need is this Part trying to manage? Acceptance? Safety? Control?

- How does this Part interact with others: aggressive, appeasing, withdrawn?

- Where did this Part first form? What age or situation is it trying to protect you from?

The goal isn't to decode the Part like a problem; it's to *understand* it like a character in your story. The better you know its voice, its fears, and its intent, the more compassion you can offer—and the more leadership you can bring.

Step 4: Welcome It: Approach with compassion and curiosity, not control. Once you recognize the Part, greet it with the voice of your SELF—not with judgment, but with curiosity. For example, "You're welcome here." "What do you need me to know?" "I see you. Thank you for protecting me."

This is often the most radical step. We are conditioned to silence or suppress our emotional reactions. But...

Parts don't soften when ignored.
They soften when seen.

Remember: You are not indulging the Part. You are including it in the system it has been working so hard to protect. You are becoming the wise adult it never had.

Step 5: Lead It: Reassure the Part, and reclaim authority. Now that you've listened, you can gently take the lead.

This is where your Authentic SELF steps forward to relieve the Part of a role it was never meant to play alone: "Thank you for trying to protect me. I've got this now. You don't have to work so hard anymore. Let me take it from here."

This is not suppression. It's reorganization. You are inviting the Part to relax, to return to its proper place—as advisor, not leader.

With time, even a few seconds of SELF-leadership during a trigger builds new neural wiring, replacing reactivity with response. Moment by moment, you're reshaping your inner system for long-term trust, freedom, and reintegration.

REAL-LIFE SCENARIOS

Triggers don't wait for your readiness. They arrive unannounced in meetings, in relationships, and in moments that seem ordinary until they suddenly aren't.

This section shows you how to work with those moments using the five-step process I laid out above. These are not theoretical situations; they're drawn from the emotional terrain most of us walk every day. The point is not to get it "right" but to recognize the doorway, to see the Part that's trying to protect you, and to respond from your SELF.

Here are 10 common examples of triggers that may activate your Parts most often:

- A boss questions your competence in front of others.

- A partner goes silent during an argument.

- You share something vulnerable and receive no response.

- You forget a deadline and feel ashamed.

- A friend leaves you out of a group gathering.

- Your child rolls their eyes and walks away.

- A colleague takes credit for your work.

- A parent criticizes your life choices (again).

- You overreact to a small mistake and feel embarrassed.

- Someone doesn't say thank you for something you gave your all to.

Each one of these moments activates a Part—usually faster than you consciously notice. I'm now going to walk you through three scenarios that will show you how to apply the five steps in the heat of life.

Scenario 1: A Boss Questions Your Work

In a team meeting, your boss raises an eyebrow and says, "This isn't what I expected from you." You freeze.

Your stomach drops. Your jaw clenches. You feel exposed. You start to spiral.

Your Wounded Overachiever—a perfection-driven Part that equates performance with worth—jumps into high alert.

And you put the five steps into action:

- Pause: You inhale slowly. You say quietly to your boss, "Let me take a moment to review that."

- Name It: You say to yourself, *A part of me is panicking. It's afraid I'm not good enough. That's my Wounded Overachiever. I recognize her well. She's always close at hand, protecting me loyally.*

- Understand It: This Part learned long ago that mistakes mean rejection. She protects by overworking and overpreparing to avoid shame.

- Welcome It: You silently say to your Part, *Thank you for showing up, dear friend. I know you're trying to keep me safe.*

- Lead It: And continue, *But, respectfully, you're wrong. I'm no longer the little girl who needs protection. We've got this. One comment doesn't define us. I'll lead the conversation from here.*

And so, you don't dissociate. You don't attack. You remain present and composed. You take the feedback without making it an identity crisis.

Scenario 2: A Partner Withdraws in an Argument

You express frustration about something small. Your partner goes quiet and becomes distant.

Your chest tightens. You feel abandoned. You start imagining worst-case outcomes.

Your Anxious Clinger—a Part that fears disconnection and rushes in to fix or cling— wants to make it all better.

And you put the five steps into action:

- Pause: You feel the urge to escalate, but instead you place a hand on your heart and breathe.

- Name It: You think, *Something in me is scared that they're pulling away. I feel a flood of panic. I recognize the familiar, terrifying grip of the Anxious Clinger. I feel my heart racing and my shoulders tightening, and I want to hold on for dear life. It feels like I am going to be left alone again.*

- Understand It: This Part learned early that silence means danger. It overcompensates by chasing reassurance.

- Welcome It: You say to your Part, *Thank you for coming to my rescue. I see you. I recognize you. You're always the first to stand up to help me.*

- Lead It: And finish, *But, respectfully, you're wrong. I'm safe right now, and strong. I'm not a needy little boy anymore. I don't need to force closeness. Let's wait with calm.*

And so, you don't pursue or accuse. You hold space for yourself and your partner. Later, you reengage from a grounded place.

Scenario 3: A Colleague Calls You Out in a Group Setting

You're in a brainstorming session. Ideas are flowing freely when a colleague abruptly says, "That's not what the client asked for," dismissing your contribution in front of the group.

You stiffen. Your eyes feel watery, but your face stays composed. You go completely quiet. Inside, you feel small, like you've disappeared.

The Icy Freezer—a hyperrational Part that freezes you into silence and submission— wants to close you down instantly. Its aim is to avoid emotional risk at all costs.

And you put the five steps into action:

- Pause: You take a quiet, full breath and sit back slightly in your chair. You gently press your feet into the ground to find your body. You say evenly, "That's a good point—let's take a closer look together."

- Name It: You think, *Something in me wants to shut down completely. That's the Icy Freezer. I clam up every time he takes over. He freezes my voice and wraps me in silence, so I won't get hurt.*

- Understand It: This Part showed up early in life, when speaking up led to ridicule or rejection. It learned to protect you by numbing emotion and withdrawing into cold silence, which felt much safer than being seen.

- Welcome It: You say to your Part, *Thank you for stepping in so quickly. I know you've always tried to keep me safe from humiliation. I appreciate you. You've done your job so faithfully.*

- Lead It: And redirect, *But, respectfully, you're wrong; I'm not under threat right now. I'm not 13, and I don't need to disappear. I'm safe enough to stay present and to speak if I choose to. I'll take it from here.*

And so, instead of going cold, you stay in the room—emotionally and relationally. You continue to contribute. Your nervous system remains engaged, not shut down. You speak up with calm confidence. You reclaim your seat at the table by your very presence.

Each of these examples reveals something essential: You are not your reaction. You are the one who notices the reaction and chooses what comes next.

That's what the practice of presence offers you: the ability to stay with yourself, no matter what.

RESISTANCE AND REPETITION

Sometimes it feels hard, and that's okay.

Not every Part will step aside gracefully. Some will resist. Some will double down. And some will pretend to cooperate while secretly keeping one hand on the wheel.

This isn't because your Parts are broken or bad; it's because they're loyal. They've been protecting your system—often for decades—and they're not convinced you can do it without them.

When a Part resists,
offer reassurance instead of reprimand.

Speak to it like an elder statesperson being honored for decades of service. Try saying, "This isn't exile. It's retirement with honor." Or, "You're not losing control. You're gaining support." Or, "You don't have to work so hard anymore." Or, "I'm not silencing you. I'm listening in a new way."

This is especially true for Parts that took on responsibility when you were very young. To them, you're still that vulnerable child. They don't yet trust that someone stronger, wiser, and more grounded is finally home.

That trust can't be demanded. It has to be earned. And you're the one who has to point it out. You need to prove that you have grown up. It's that simple, really.

At first, this process may feel clunky or artificial. You may pause long after the moment has passed. You may forget your steps, mix them up, or freeze entirely. That's okay.

In the beginning, this work happens in slow motion—after the fact, in the aftermath, during reflection. But with time and repetition, something beautiful happens: The steps come quicker. Your awareness sharpens. Your reaction becomes a response, and then the space between trigger and response begins to widen. Eventually, you notice the arrival of the Part *in the moment*. And one day, you catch it *before* it happens; you're able preempt the hijacking. The Part still rises, but it doesn't take over. Then, finally, the process moves back into the subconscious, repatterned by trust. You don't even notice that you're now fluidly handling difficult situations from your powerful SELF.

This is neuroplasticity in action. Your inner world is learning that the SELF can lead.

And every time you show up—even imperfectly—you build credibility as a leader. Consistency creates safety. And safety creates change.

WHEN IT DOESN'T WORK

Despite your best intentions, there will be days when it doesn't work.

You'll know the steps. You'll have the language. And still, in the moment, a Part will hijack the system—and you'll snap, spiral, shut down, or say something you regret.

This is not a failure. It's a sign that something in you is overwhelmed, overtaxed, or just plain tired.

Stress, fatigue, illness: These don't just wear down your body. They fray the link to your SELF. When your system is under strain, Parts get louder, faster, and more insistent. That's not weakness; that's biology. Your brain senses your more vulnerable condition, and your sub-personalities rally to protect you.

In those moments, you won't always be able to pause and reflect. You may only realize after the fact that a Part was leading. That's okay. Even that awareness—late, messy, and imperfect as it may be—is a movement toward reintegration.

Remember:

This is not a performance. It's a practice.

What matters most is not getting it right every time. What matters is returning without shame, reaching for the tools again, and asking the question, "Who was driving just now?"

Micro-moments of presence have profound impact. One breath, one question, one act of curiosity in the aftermath of reactivity: These are the building blocks of SELF-leadership.

Think of it like a muscle. It grows through use, especially when it's hard and you feel like giving up. That's when the real work happens.

Be gentle with yourself. You are learning a new way of being. Every honest attempt is enough.

DAILY REINTEGRATION

Transformation doesn't happen in grand gestures. It happens in the quiet, daily rhythm of returning to yourself.

The real power of this work lies not in single breakthroughs but in consistent, compassionate presence. Moment by moment, you are retraining your system to recognize your SELF as the natural leader. And, like any leadership, it takes practice.

Below are a few gentle rituals and routines that support ongoing reintegration. Choose what works for you. Adapt them. Make them yours. This is about building a life that supports your inner harmony.

Begin the day by asking, "Who's driving right now?" This one question invites awareness before autopilot takes over. It doesn't require fixing anything—just noticing. If you wake up with anxiety, maybe the Frantic Fixer is already at the wheel. If you feel numb, perhaps the Icy Freezer has stepped in. Simply naming who's present begins the process of returning you to your SELF.

Turn your Parts into pen pals. Write to them directly: *Hello, Exhausted Achiever. What are you protecting me from today?* Or, *Dear Angry Protector, I'm listening. What do you need me to know?* Let them respond on the page. Don't overthink it. Don't try to sound wise. Just write. Over time, you'll begin to hear clearer voices and build deeper trust.

Use stillness to listen. Even a few minutes of stillness can help you differentiate your SELF from the noise within. Meditation is about space. Try sitting quietly and scanning your internal world: *What Parts are present right now?* And, *Can I sit with them without reacting?* You don't need to change anything. Just witness. That, in itself, is leadership.

Engage the power of your body. Parts live in the mind but are connected with the body. When you feel stuck in their narrative, move. Walk. Stretch. Breathe deeply. Step into nature. Let the wind or sun or stillness of a tree reregulate your nervous system. Embodied practices help bring your SELF back online. They remind you that presence is not only a mental state but a physical one.

Check in before bed. Before sleep, look back: *Where did I lead from SELF today? Or, Where did a Part step in, and what was it trying to protect?* This is for curiosity, not judgment. Even a single moment of awareness strengthens your inner system.

Call a meeting. Once a week—or whenever you feel internal friction—gather your inner team. Close your eyes. Picture your Parts seated around a table. Call the meeting to order. Listen to what each voice has to say. Then speak as the chairperson: "Thank you all for being here. I've heard you. I'm taking the lead now." This imaginative ritual brings coherence to your inner world. It's where leadership becomes lived.

Whatever your practice looks like, keep it gentle. Keep it kind. And above all, keep it yours.

Presence is not a performance. It's a way of coming home.

MOMENT BY MOMENT

This is where your practice takes root: in the real-time triggers of life. In hallway conversations and hard mornings. In moments when you remember, even briefly, that there's a different way to meet what's rising in you.

Transformation rarely arrives in a single, sweeping epiphany. More often, it unfolds in the quiet moments you choose to pause, to breathe, and to lead from your SELF rather than your Parts. These micro-acts of presence are the architecture of a new life.

In the next chapter, we'll take an in-depth look at five of my favorite Parts. My hope is that visualizing them will help inspire and aid you as you introduce your SELF to your own committee of sub-personalities.

CHAPTER 6

Familiar Patterns

It can be very difficult to identify the voices that have been shouting in your head for most of your life. So, in this chapter we'll explore some commonly occurring Parts. I hope you enjoy meeting these intriguing characters on paper. More importantly, I hope that they will inspire you to seek out and name your own cast of sub-personalities. In doing so, you will learn how to appreciate and gently thank them, even as you take back authority over them.

First, let me offer an important reflection:

You are not alone in your experience.

As unique as your inner landscape may feel—and as unique as the exact experiences and events of your life certainly are—the voices within you echo in the hearts and minds of others across every culture, profession, and path.

Here are a few of these familiar inner figures, sub-personalities that quietly shape how we think, feel, and protect ourselves.

Each one is a real sub-personality from one of my clients, and you may recognize them from your own cast of characters. They are not evidence of your brokenness. They are signs that you are human—beautifully, protectively, imperfectly human. Seeing them clearly is not just a comfort. It is the beginning of compassion.

THE SELFLESS PLEASER

The Selfless Pleaser's goal is connection at any cost. She wants to keep you safe through approval. She believes that being liked—being agreeable, adaptable, and easy—is the best way to avoid conflict, disappointment, or exclusion. Her strategy is to become who "they" need so that, maybe, they'll stay.

She emerged in early childhood, when love felt conditional, based on your behavior, your usefulness, or your emotional tone. You learned that displeasing others brought tension or withdrawal. So, you adapted. You became pleasant, predictable, and perpetually available.

Her rallying cry is, "Just say yes. Don't upset them. They might leave. Keep them happy—even if it costs you. Be what they need. Then there's a place for you here."

Her charm is disarming, but it comes at a price. You lose track of your own preferences, boundaries, and needs. Relationships feel lopsided, and resentment simmers beneath the smile. Over time, she creates an identity built on accommodation—leaving your Authentic SELF unseen, unchosen, and quietly aching.

You can say back, "I am allowed to have needs. I am worthy of them. I am lovable, regardless. I can disappoint someone and still be loved. I don't need to earn belonging—it's my birthright."

THE COLD DEBT COLLECTOR

The Cold Debt Collector wants you to be safe from rejection and invisibility. His strategy is to ensure that your goodness is visible, remembered, and reciprocated. Every helpful act is recorded—silently—with the unspoken expectation that it will earn you a return. Loyalty. Gratitude. Protection. In his mind, that's only fair.

He came online early, in a world where care wasn't consistently offered freely. Somewhere in your young nervous system, you learned that if you gave enough—performed enough, served enough—someone might stay. Or see you. Or stop hurting you. You became the caretaker to survive and the recordkeeper to matter.

His refrain is, "Don't forget what you did for them. They owe you. Keep score. It's the only way to protect yourself. If they don't repay you, they don't respect you. Don't let them get away with that."

His approach may appear generous, but it's transactional at its core. It creates a subtle atmosphere of emotional debt, which breeds distance. Others feel unseen and unloved. Relationships become contracts. Even when you give, you feel unfulfilled because it's never quite enough. And when repayment doesn't come, you withdraw, quietly hurt, carrying the loneliness of your own unspoken terms.

You can contend, "I give because it's who I am, not because I expect a return. I am enough. I don't need to keep the books anymore—we are not in debt. We are in relationship."

The Silent Martyr

The Silent Martyr wants you to be good. Pure. Above reproach. Her strategy is quiet suffering, absorbing burdens without complaint, hoping that your self-sacrifice will earn you love and protection, or at least prevent rejection. She believes that enduring silently is the highest form of strength, a thankless devotion.

She was born in a world where expressing needs led to conflict, punishment, or abandonment. You learned early that voicing discomfort was dangerous or futile. So, you stayed quiet. You carried others' pain as if it were your own, hoping that someone might notice your goodness—and finally care for you in return.

She whispers, "Don't make a scene. Don't burden anyone. Just carry it. Don't expect appreciation. They won't understand, and it won't help. Just get through it. If you're good enough, they'll eventually see how much you've done for them."

Her devotion can feel noble, even saintly—but it isolates you. Your silence creates confusion, not connection. People don't see your needs because you've hidden them. You become resentful, exhausted, and emotionally invisible. Over time, your unspoken hope curdles into bitterness when no one comes to rescue the one who never asked for help. Even when they offer words of appreciation, you don't know what to do with them, making them uncomfortable. So, your effort becomes truly thankless.

You can rebut her, "I can be loved and still have limits. My voice matters. I matter. I can speak my needs without guilt. This is strength, too."

The Pessimistic Prophet

The Pessimistic Prophet wants to shield you from disappointment by lowering your expectations. He believes that, if you expect the worst, you can't be hurt. His gift is foresight—used not to inspire but to prepare for collapse.

He emerged in a world where hope was punished, things often went wrong, and optimism was met with pain or humiliation. You learned that it was safer to scan for danger than to trust in possibility. It was better to brace than to break.

He warns, "Don't get your hopes up. You know that things seldom, if ever, work out. People always leave. Nothing changes. If you expect less, you'll hurt less. Don't waste your time dreaming. If anything good happens, it's only by luck...and you're not lucky...only *they* are."

His protection dulls your life. Anticipating failure, you hold back your gifts, mute your desires, and undercut your potential. His predictions feel like wisdom, but they narrow your world. You stop risking, stop reaching, and stop dreaming. And slowly, you forget what you're capable of.

But you can counter, "I hear your concern. But preparing for pain is not the same as being free from it. I am strong enough to hope and resilient enough to recover, whatever comes. When something good happens, I deserve it. I have worked hard for it, and deserve it."

THE DUTIFUL DAUGHTER

The Dutiful Daughter wants to keep you aligned with expectation, to preserve harmony, avoid shame, and stay "good" in the eyes of those you once depended on. Her purpose is obedience cloaked in loyalty. She believes that doing what's expected, not what's true, is the price of love.

She was shaped in a system where roles were rigid and approval was earned through compliance. You learned that questioning, expressing, or straying from the script brought disapproval or rupture. So, you made yourself small, consistently reliable, and quiet—a keeper of the peace, even at your own expense. And you worked very hard to get this right.

She insists, "Don't disappoint them. Do what's right, even if it's not real. This is who we are. Don't rock the boat. If they see the real you, they'll be disappointed and may turn away. You'll be left alone, as you probably deserve."

Her devotion can feel virtuous, but it locks you into borrowed values. You lose touch with your Authentic SELF: your voice, your longings, your fire. Life becomes a performance of inherited roles, not a true expression of who you are. Beneath the polished exterior, grief gathers.

Argue with her, "I honor where I came from, but I no longer belong to those expectations. I am worthy of love and respect, regardless. Even in my worst performance, I am worthy. I belong to myself now—and I get to choose."

OTHER CHARACTERS

Here is a short list of some other favorite sub-personalities that I have met, respected, and grown to love in my client work:

- The Anxious Planner
- The Blind Rager
- The Callous Critic
- The Devoted Workaholic
- The Echoing Apologizer
- The Ever-Ready Rescuer
- The Frantic Fixer
- The Jittery Joker
- The Polished Performer
- The Relentless Achiever
- The Restless Sentry
- The Rigid Rule-Keeper
- The Smiling Pretender
- The Stoic Provider

We all carry familiar strangers inside us. What matters now is not how many you have or how loudly they speak but how you relate to them. The moment you recognize these Parts with warmth instead of judgment, you begin to soften the patterns that once felt unmovable. And in that softening, space opens: a space where you can listen, lead, and live from something deeper than survival. This is how you begin to reclaim quiet authority over the algorithms that have long shaped your inner world—leading not from fear but from clarity, compassion, and choice. May these portraits remind you that you are never alone. We are all walking each other home, one Part at a time.

RIPPLES

You now hold the tools. You know how to recognize a Part, how to greet it, and how to respond with care instead of control. This doesn't mean you'll never be triggered. It just means you'll know how to return.

And something beautiful happens when you do: The people around you feel the shift. Your children notice the calm in your voice. Your partner senses the space you've made for both of you. Your team registers a deeper steadiness. Presence doesn't just change you. It changes everything you touch.

This work begins inside—but it doesn't stay there.

In the final chapter, we'll explore how healing ripples outward, magically: how your personal transformation creates relational safety, emotional intelligence, and collective change. The journey continues, not just within you but without.

CHAPTER 7

PASS IT ON

You've come a long way. You've mapped your mind. You've met your Parts. You've stepped into the quiet, consistent practice of SELF-leadership. But this work—profound as it is—was never meant to stop with you.

Personal transformation is deeply intimate, but it is never just personal. Healing is relational. When you begin to lead from your Authentic SELF, the atmosphere around you shifts. A kind of gravity emerges. Tension dissolves. The nervous systems of others begin to calibrate, mirroring your calm and resonating with your presence.

This is the ripple effect.

The more SELF-led individuals we have in the world, the more capacity we have for connected families, compassionate teams, resilient communities, and wise leadership. Your healing brings a subtle coherence into spaces that may have long been fragmented.

It's not magic. It's mirror neurons.

Science shows that our brains are wired to resonate with the emotional states of those around us.[24] This is why anxiety is contagious—and so is calm. Your steadiness can stabilize a room. Your choice to respond instead of react sets a tone that others begin to trust. Quietly, consistently, your internal work becomes external safety.

You don't need to raise your voice to lead. You just need to anchor in your SELF. You need to speak with your authentic voice more.

And as your inner world grows more coherent, its influence begins to radiate outward, transforming not just how you feel but how you are felt by others. Your inner peace becomes a shared light.

Like concentric circles on water, your inner alignment extends outward, touching every environment you inhabit. From the deeply personal to the quietly societal, your presence reshapes the spaces around you.

At the core, your inner world becomes less volatile. You notice your Parts more quickly. You soothe them with compassion. You manage them with authority. You navigate life with more clarity and less reactivity. The internal noise softens. Harmony emerges.

Then, your presence becomes a haven for others. Conflict de-escalates in your company. Loved ones feel safer, not because you've changed them but because you've changed how you meet them. Your children absorb your calm. Your colleagues lean into your steadiness. You offer space.

And finally, when individuals practice SELF-leadership, social circles begin to shift. Culture changes when people bring consciousness into their choices. Healing ripples through relationships, communities, and generations.

The path to a more compassionate world starts here, in you.

You don't need to preach. You don't need to convince anyone. By remaining steady in your own presence, like a lighthouse on the rocky shore of a wild ocean, you quietly become a beacon for others. To live as a lighthouse means you stop chasing and stand in your own light. You remain rooted in calm, clarity, and compassion. You lead not with volume but with presence.

And, in your stillness, others begin to see more clearly.

Your clarity gives others permission to be curious. Your courage allows them to soften. When one person sees clearly, it helps others remember their own light.

You might share what you've learned. But, even more powerfully, you'll embody it—in the way you parent, partner, lead, and love.

Be patient. Not everyone will trust your new presence right away. That's okay. Hold your ground gently. Let them feel the difference. Over time, they'll begin to believe what your nervous system already knows: Safety is possible.

¤ ¤ ¤ ¤ ¤

As we close, I ask this of you: Let the change you make be more than your story. Let it become a quiet offering, an invitation for others to begin their own journey to reintegration.

If something in you has stirred—if you've seen even a flicker of truth in these words—don't keep it to yourself. Share it through your tranquil radiance.

Let your life become a transmission. Let your presence be the invitation. You don't need to start a movement. Just be a light.

Let this not be the end of your journey but the beginning of someone else's.

IDENTIFYING PARTS THROUGH TRIGGERS: A PRACTICAL GUIDE

One of the most powerful ways to meet your Parts is through the very moments that provoke you. Triggers—those emotional spikes or sudden inner storms—are rarely random. They are reliable messengers, pointing toward a Part that is active, overwhelmed, or trying to protect something vulnerable. Here's a step-by-step guide to help you use real-life moments to map your inner system.

Step 1: Recall a recent trigger. Think of a moment when you felt emotionally reactive: frustrated, ashamed, panicked, or withdrawn. Choose a situation that still holds a charge, even if mild. The more honest you are, the more insight you'll gain.

Step 2: Describe the situation. What exactly happened? Where were you? Who was involved? What words were said? Be specific. This isn't about judgment; it's about context. Clarity here lays the foundation for deeper insight.

Step 3: Name the emotion(s). What did you feel in the moment? Anger? Fear? Shame? Sadness? Try to identify the core feeling beneath any immediate reaction. If you felt "annoyed," was it actually disappointment or rejection?

Step 4: Track the reaction. What did you do, think, or say in response? Did you lash out, shut down, try to fix, or flee? Notice both the outer behavior and the inner narrative that unfolded.

Step 5: Listen for the voice. What was the voice in your head saying? Did it sound urgent, critical, fearful, or controlling? Try to quote it directly; this helps the Part begin to take shape in the theatre of your imagination.

Step 6: Imagine the Part. Close your eyes. Ask yourself, *Who might be feeling this? What does this Part look like? What does it sound like? How old does it feel?* Let your imagination assist you. This is about being authentic, not accurate.

Step 7: Ask questions. Get to know the Part:

- What is this Part trying to protect?

- What does it need?

- How long has it been doing this job?

These questions gently uncover the Part's intention and origin—without shame or resistance.

Step 8: Apply the three-step response. Once the Part is revealed, you can respond with grounded leadership:

- Thank you for protecting me.

- Respectfully, you're wrong; this isn't the same situation.

- I've got this. I'm here now, and I'm leading.

This small dialogue often brings immense relief, both to the Part and to the system as a whole.

Remember, you don't need to identify every Part at once. Start with the ones that arise most often or most intensely. Over time, a mosaic of your inner cast will emerge organically, as you build trust with your inner world.

ILLUSTRATOR'S NOTE

The familiar collaboration between artist and writer has arrived this time at the notion of imposter syndrome. As I embarked upon my creative analysis of the topic, I thought carefully about the concept of *truth in existence*, whereby the identity of a person must manifest itself wholly in their truth, not from external value systems but from embracing the untidiness of being. I felt confronted by my own authenticity and how much of myself I *perform* instead of *allow*. Not unlike you and I, Daniel and his comrades struggle with the bittersweet performance of life.

The artworks in this book are designed to develop stylistically alongside Daniel's experience of imposterism. I use the motif of light to distort and reinvert identity. We find that the artworks begin as glorified corporate masquerades. Stage-lit scenes with backlit characters produce a fictitious atmosphere of power. As we approach the watershed of the story, each character opens up in a display of vulnerability. The compositions shift to an intimate disposition, kissed by natural light. The characters develop into individuals, and we are not left with a weakened image of them but rather with depth and veracity.

Another prominent motif presents itself in paper sheets. The falling sheets subtly refer to the disruption and reorganization of knowledge. Retaining the corporate tone of the setting, these items imagine the path traveled in reorganizing one's identity in the presence of newfound personal knowledge.

As the artist, it is my job to give momentum to Roddy's words through my concepts, process, and medium. We decided on the medium of oil, a bright and viscous paint that depicts in brilliant color these ideas.

I understand very clearly one of Roddy's priorities in this book series: The problem is *never* without a solution or, as he would call it, hope. I have tried to capture the soft luminance of hope even in the presence of reservation.

In life, we encounter the challenges of our own authenticity as it is mounted against the backdrop of our environment. We often muddle the essence of our truth with childish methodology. The performance of life can be daunting, but seeking refuge in a cast of characters constructed in the very vulnerable period of our youth cannot sustain the belief that we are enough. Know that this book is a tool for you to accomplish the tasks of upliftment, fulfillment, and truth in existence.

CONNECT

You can visit me at my website, www.RoddyCarter.com. There, you will find more of my work that is designed to help you on your journey to reintegration, along with my recommendations for additional reading and research. Please reach out to me directly at connect@RoddyCarter.com to share your victories and struggles.

> If this book resonated with you, I'd be honored if you'd leave a review on the site where you purchased it...your voice helps others find it.

FURTHER READING

Should you wish to delve further into PMM concepts, I invite you to explore the resources provided below:

- *The Archetypes and the Collective Unconscious*, Carl G. Jung – A seminal text in analytical psychology that lays out the theory of universal psychic patterns (archetypes) and their formative influence on human experience

- *Awakening the Heroes Within: Twelve Archetypes to Help Us Find Ourselves and Transform Our World*, Carol S. Pearson – A rich, accessible exploration of 12 universal archetypes that shape the human journey, offering a road map for personal growth, self-understanding, and mythic transformation

- *The Body Keeps the Score: Brain, Mind, and Body in the Healing of Trauma*, Bessel van der Kolk – A foundational work on trauma and how the body stores emotional memory

- *The Brain That Changes Itself: Stories of Personal Triumph From the Frontiers of Brain Science*, Norman Doidge – A powerful explanation of neuroplasticity, showing how the brain adapts and heals

- *Embracing Our Selves: The Voice Dialogue Manual*, Hal Stone and Sidra L. Stone – A pioneering introduction to Voice Dialogue that unveils the diverse inner selves that shape our choices, behavior, and relationships

- *Man and His Symbols*, Carl G. Jung – Jung's most accessible work, introducing the collective unconscious and archetypes through vivid case studies and rich, symbolic language

- *Mindsight: The New Science of Personal Transformation*, Daniel J. Siegel – A groundbreaking guide to integrating brain science and mindfulness, helping readers develop awareness of their inner world to foster healing and growth

- *The Mosaic Mind: Empowering the Tormented Selves of Child Abuse Survivors*, Regina A. Goulding and Richard C. Schwartz – A trauma-sensitive guide to Internal Family Systems therapy, offering gentle techniques for working with dissociative parts and complex inner systems

- *No Bad Parts: Healing Trauma and Restoring Wholeness With the Internal Family Systems Model*, Richard C. Schwartz – A clear, gentle introduction to Internal Family Systems, aligned with PMM's respect for all Parts

- *Radical Acceptance: Embracing Your Life With the Heart of a Buddha*, Tara Brach – A tender and profound call to embrace every part of ourselves with mindful compassion

- *The Untethered Soul: The Journey Beyond Yourself*, Michael A. Singer – An elegant invitation to become the observer of your inner world, echoing PMM's perspective on the SELF

NOTES

1   Jung, C. G. (1981). *The archetypes and the collective unconscious* (R. F. C. Hull, Trans.). Princeton University Press. (Original work published 1934–1950)

2   Perls, F., Hefferline, R. F., & Goodman, P. (1980). *Gestalt therapy*. Bantam Books.

3   van der Kolk, B. (2015). *The body keeps the score*. Penguin Books.

4   Stone, H., & Stone, S. L. (1998). *Embracing our selves: The voice dialogue manual*. New World Library.

5   Goulding, R. A., & Schwartz, R. C. (1995). *The mosaic mind: Empowering the tormented selves of child abuse survivors*. W. W. Norton & Company.

6   Schwartz, R. C. (2023). *Introduction to internal family systems*. Sounds True.

7   Ackerman, S. (1992.) *Discovering the brain*. National Academies Press.

8   Zimmer, C. (2011, January 1). 100 trillion connections: New efforts probe and map the brain's detailed architecture. *Scientific American*. https://www.scientificamerican.com/article/100-trillion-connections/

9   Center on the Developing Child. (2007). *In brief: The science of early childhood development*. Harvard University. https://developingchild.harvard.edu/resources/inbriefs/inbrief-science-of-ecd/

10   Sakai, J. (2020). Core concept: How synaptic pruning shapes neural wiring during development and, possibly, in disease. *Proceedings of the National Academy of Sciences of the United States of America, 117*(28), 16096–16099. https://doi.org/10.1073/pnas.2010281117

11   Dutta, D. J., Woo, D. H., Lee, P. R., Pajevic, S., Bukalo, O., Huffman, W. C., Wake, H., Basser, P. J., SheikhBahaei, S., Lazarevic, V., Smith, J. C., & Fields, R. D. (2018). Regulation of myelin structure and conduction velocity by perinodal astrocytes. *Proceedings of the National Academy of Sciences of the United States of America, 115*(46), 11832–11837. https://doi.org/10.1073/pnas.1811013115

12   Waxman, S. G. (1980). Determinants of conduction velocity in myelinated nerve fibers. *Muscle & Nerve, 3*(2), 141–150. https://doi.org/10.1002/mus.880030207

13   Šimic, G., Tkalcic, M., Vukic, V., Mulc, D., Španic, E., Šagud, M., Olucha-Bordonau, F. E., Vukšic, M., & Hof, P. R. (2021). Understanding emotions: Origins and roles of the amygdala. *Biomolecules, 11*(6), 823. https://doi.org/10.3390/biom11060823

14   Malivoire, B. L., Girard, T. A., Patel, R., & Monson, C. M. (2018). Functional connectivity of hippocampal subregions in PTSD: Relations with symptoms. *BMC Psychiatry, 18*, 129. https://doi.org/10.1186/s12888-018-1716-9

15   SAMHSA. (2014). *Trauma-informed care in behavioral health services*. Substance Abuse and Mental Health Services Administration.

16 Fox, S. E., Levitt, P., & Nelson III, C. A. (2010). How the timing and quality of early experiences influence the development of brain architecture. *Child Development, 81*(1), 28–40. https://doi.org/10.1111/j.1467-8624.2009.01380.x

17 Ibid.

18 Ibid.

19 SAMHSA. (2014). *Trauma-informed care in behavioral health services.* Substance Abuse and Mental Health Services Administration.

20 Ibid.

21 Ladkin, D., Spiller, C., & Craze, G. (2018). The journey of individuation: A Jungian alternative to the theory and practice of leading authentically. *Leadership, 14*(4), 415–434. https://doi.org/10.1177/1742715016681942

22 Dutta, D. J., Woo, D. H., Lee, P. R., Pajevic, S., Bukalo, O., Huffman, W. C., Wake, H., Basser, P. J., SheikhBahaei, S., Lazarevic, V., Smith, J. C., & Fields, R. D. (2018). Regulation of myelin structure and conduction velocity by perinodal astrocytes. *Proceedings of the National Academy of Sciences of the United States of America, 115*(46), 11832–11837. https://doi.org/10.1073/pnas.1811013115

23 Carroll, J. (2020). Imagination, the brain's default mode network, and imaginative verbal artifacts. In J. Carroll, M. Clasen, & E. Jonsson (Eds.), *Evolutionary perspectives on imaginative culture* (pp. 31–52). Springer. https://doi.org/10.1007/978-3-030-46190-4-2

24 Trieu, M., Foster, A. E., Yaseen, Z. S., Beaubian, C., & Calati, R. (2019). Neurobiology of empathy. In A. E. Foster & Z. S. Yaseen (Eds.), *Teaching empathy in healthcare* (pp. 17–39). Springer.

For more information, visit www.RoddyCarter.com,

or reach out directly via connect@RoddyCarter.com.